EASY TO MAKE
SOFT TOYS

EASY TO MAKE
SOFT TOYS

Cheryl Owen

Series consultant: Eve Harlow

BROCKHAMPTON PRESS
LONDON

First published in Great Britain in 1991
by Anaya Publishers Ltd, Strode House,
44-50 Osnaburgh Street, London NW1 3ND

Copyright © Collins & Brown 1996

This edition published 1996 by Brockhampton Press,
a member of Hodder Headline PLC Group

Editor Eve Harlow
Design by Design 23
Photography Di Lewis
Illustrator Kate Simunek
Patterns Mike Leaman

British Library Cataloguing in Publication Data

Owen, Cheryl
Easy soft toys.–(Easy to make).
1. Toymaking. Toymaking
I. Title. II. Series

ISBN 1-86019-103-7

Typeset by Tradespools Limited, Frome, Somerset, UK
Colour reproduction by Columbia Offset, Singapore
Printed and bound in EC

CONTENTS

Introduction

Toymaking is a fascinating hobby and a craft that can be learned by anyone who can sew a little. Only basic sewing equipment is required and the techniques necessary for successful toymaking are described in this chapter.

Handmade toys are extra special and in this book you will find a complete menagerie of creatures to make to delight any child – or adult!

There are projects for all abilities whether you are new to toy-making or an accomplished needleworker. A knowledge of sewing is useful but not essential as the instructions and patterns are very easy to follow. Before you begin, read the details on equipment, materials and techniques so that you are familiar with the methods used.

Equipment

You will need the usual equipment associated with sewing – pins, needles, scissors, tape measure and thread.

Pins and needles

Pins are easily lost in the pile of fur fabric so glass or plastic headed types are best because they are easier to see. Count the number of pins used at each stage to be sure that none have been left in a toy. You will need a range of hand-sewing and embroidery needles plus a bodkin for turning narrow tubes of fabric.

Scissors

Keep three pairs of scissors on hand for toy-making – an old pair for cutting card and paper, dressmaking scissors for cutting fabrics and a small pair for cutting threads and small shapes from felt.

Pens and pencils

Use an HB pencil or quick-drying waterproof pen for marking patterns on the wrong side of fabric.

Toymaking fabrics

A wide range of fabrics, fur fabric and felt, suitable for toymaking are readily available from fabric and needlecraft shops. Some can be obtained from specialist mail order companies and a list of these is on page 96. Most fur fabrics have a knitted backing which makes them easy to work with as they will stretch but do not fray.

Filling

Make sure the toy filling you use meets with the current safety standards. This will be noted on the packaging. Use the best filling you can afford – Dacron and polyester is very good. It is bulky and springy and is washable. Kapok, although luxuriously soft, is not suitable as it is not washable. Do not use foam chips for filling toys as they are dangerous to children and also make lumpy toys. Use plastic granules for bean bags such as the lion. Dried peas or rice can be used but remember that toys filled with these cannot be washed until the filling has been removed.

Toy-making components

The size of eyes and noses makes all the difference to a toy animal's appeal. Facial features and joints can be bought in craft and haberdashery shops or by mail order. The components must meet with toy-making safety standards and this will be marked on any packaging.

BASIC TECHNIQUES

Graph patterns

Most of the patterns in this book are given as graph patterns, with a scale of 1 square = 1in (2.5cm). Copy the patterns line for line on dressmakers squared paper with 1in (2.5cm) squares then re-trace the patterns. Use thin, fairly transparent paper for pattern making. Tracing paper is not suitable as it is too stiff and tears easily. Simple shapes like squares and rectangles can be drawn directly onto the fabric.

Inserting a safety
eye through fabric.

Safety eyes and noses

Many of the toys in this book have plastic safety eyes. To attach these, make a tiny hole through the fabric at the eye position with the point of a small pair of scissors. From the right side, insert the stalk of the eye through the hole then push the washer onto the stalk as far as it will go, working from the wrong side. On some toys, the stalk is inserted through a felt 'iris' before being attached. Do not use buttons for eyes if the toy is intended for a very young child. Plastic safety noses are applied in the same way as eyes.

Jointed limb unit
inserted through fabric.

Jointed limbs

The squirrel, fox and dinosaur (pages 30, 36 and 56), have jointed limbs. To attach these, make a small hole at the joint position. From the inside of the arms and legs, push the stalk of the joint through the hole then stuff the limbs. Insert the stalk through to the inside of the body then push the washer on firmly.

Cutting out

When a pattern says 'place to the fold', fabric and felt should be folded in half and the pattern lined up with the folded edge. If the piece is to be cut in fur, fold the pattern paper in half, draw the pattern against the fold then cut out from the doubled paper. Open the pattern flat.

When bias strips are to be cut, cut across the fabric diagonally.

Seam allowances

Throughout the book these are ¼in (6mm) unless stated otherwise. Seams are stitched with right sides facing unless you are instructed differently.

Making a start

Use a lot of pins when pinning pile fabric seams as the two fur surfaces tend to move apart. Match pattern markings – dots, notches and foldlines. It is a good idea to baste seams before stitching. You may find it simpler to hand sew where seams meet – for example on gussets.

After stitching

Snip into the seam allowance on curved seams and trim away excess fabric at corners. Also snip the seam allowance at inverted corners. If the fabric type allows, press seams open. Use a needle to pull out any fur trapped in the seams. When the edge of a fur piece has to be turned to the inside, trim the pile on the seam allowance close to the backing fabric.

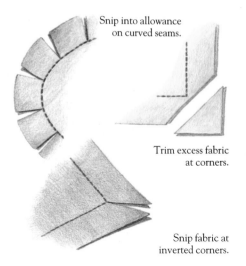

Snip into allowance
on curved seams.

Trim excess fabric
at corners.

Snip fabric at
inverted corners.

thread and make a small stitch at the place
to be marked, leaving a thread end of about
1½in (4cm). Make another stitch at the
same point, leaving a 2in (5cm) loop and cut
the thread with a 1½in (4cm) end. Pull away
the pattern and part the fabric pieces
slightly. Cut the threads between the
fabric layers.

Use tailor's tacks
to mark positions.

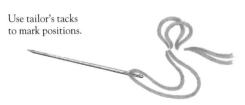

Back stitch
Use back stitch to hand sew seams (below).

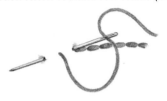

Slip stitch
Use slip stitch to join one or two folded
edges. Bring the needle out through a folded
edge and insert through the opposite fold for
¼in (6mm). Bring out the needle and insert
back along the first fold.

Ladder stitch
If the fabric has been slashed to turn right
side out, close the gap with ladder stitch.
Bring the needle to the right side ⅛in (3mm)
from the gap, make a stitch over the gap and
insert the needle to the wrong side, make a
¼in (6mm) stitch along side the gap then
make a stitch again across the gap.

Whiskers
Toy-making whiskers are lengths of horse
hair. To attach the whiskers, bring the
needle out to the right side at the whisker
position. Bend a bunch of whiskers in half
making a loop and insert the needle through
the loop. Insert the needle back through the
point where it emerged pulling the whiskers
against the face. Bring the needle out on the
opposite side of the face and attach another
bunch in the same way.

Attaching bunches
of whiskers to
toy's face.

Work ladder stitch
to close gaps.

STITCHES USED IN TOYMAKING

Tailor's tacks
Use tailor's tacks to mark positions that are
to be matched, such as darts on double layers
of fabric.

   With the pattern still pinned in place,
thread a needle with a doubled length of

Embroidery stitches
A few stitches are used in making the toys in
this book – stem stitch, satin stitch, fly stitch
and French knots.

9

ONE

Around the Farm

Daisy the cow

This large-sized toy could make a comfortable play-seat for a small child but it is a cuddly friend also for an older boy or girl.

Materials

1yd (90cm) of 60in (150cm)-wide chestnut polished fur fabric

20in (50cm) of 60in (150cm)-wide white polished fur fabric

8in (20cm) of 54in (137cm)-wide white long hair fur fabric

12in (30cm) of 60in (150cm)-wide peach felt

8in (20cm) of 60in (150cm)-wide fawn felt

Scraps of white, brown, blue, black and yellow felt

Washable polyester toy filling

Preparation

1 Draw a pattern from the graph pattern on pages 14–15 on squared paper. Put in all marks, words and numerals. Cut out the pattern pieces and use them to cut 2 heads and 4 ears from chestnut-coloured fur. From the same fur, cut 4 legs on the fold. From white fur, cut 1 gusset on the fold. Cut an oval for the cow's fringe 8in × 6in (20 × 15cm) from white long hair fur. From the same fur, cut a tail tip 4 × 3in (10 × 7.5cm) with the fur pile running along the piece.

2 From peach felt, cut 1 muzzle on the fold. From white felt, cut 2 eyes and 1 daisy. From brown felt, cut 2 irises. From blue felt, cut 2 eyelids, from black, cut 2 sets of eyelashes, 2 nostrils. From yellow felt, cut 1 daisy centre. From fawn felt cut 4 hooves on the fold.

3 From chestnut fur, cut a strip 10 × 2in (25 × 5cm) for the tail, an oval shape for the base 14½in (37cm) long × 11in (28cm) wide and a large oval 28in (71cm) long × 24in (62cm) wide for the body, cutting the fur with the pile running along the pieces.

Making the toy

4 Stitch the long edges of the tail and the tip together making 2 tubes and use a bodkin to turn the tail right side out.

Turn the tail right side out

Stage 6: Baste the tail and legs to the base.

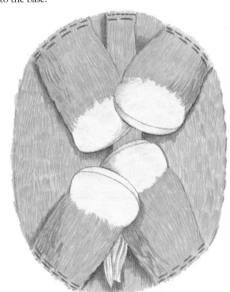

Stage 8: Baste ears between triangles on head darts.

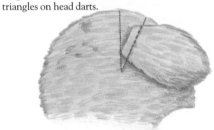

12

5 Use the bodkin to pull the tail through the tail tip. Pin the top of the tail tip level with the bottom of the tail and stitch across the end through all the thicknesses. Pull the tail tip down to the right side, baste the top of the tail to one end of the oval base piece.

6 Fold the legs and hooves in half, stitch along the long edges of the legs A–B and the un-notched edges of the hooves B–C. Stitch the hooves to the legs B–B. Turn and stuff. Baste legs across the top then to the base, 10in (25cm) apart, on the long edges.

7 Gather the circumference of the oval body piece. Pin to the base with the pile of the fur running towards the tail. Pull up the gathers to fit the base and stitch, leaving an opening to turn. Turn right side out and stuff firmly. Hand sew the opening closed.

8 Stitch the ears together leaving the ends open. Turn to the right side and baste along the seam allowance between the triangles on the head darts. Stitch the darts then stitch the gusset between the heads D–E.

9 Fold the tucks on the muzzle and baste across the edges. Stitch the muzzle to the head F–D–D–F. Stuff the head firmly, turn under the lower edges and hand sew securely to the body.

10 On the fringe oval, cut the pile level on the short ends. Gather the oval a little and pin to the top of the head with the pile toward the front. Hand sew in place.

11 Pin the eyes and nostrils to the head. Pin the irises and lids in place and cut a fringe along the lashes. Pin the lashes to the eyes. Hand sew all the pieces in position and gently lift the lashes upwards. Pin the daisy and centre in front of the right ear and sew in position.

trace off actual size

Trace these pieces and cut them from felt.

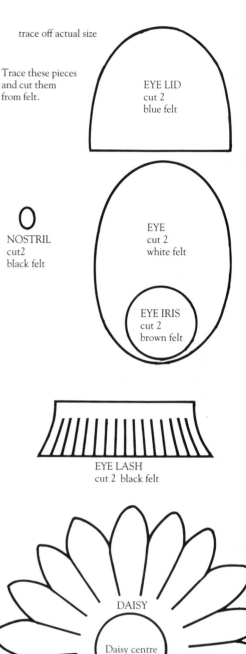

NOSTRIL
cut2
black felt

EYE LID
cut 2
blue felt

EYE
cut 2
white felt

EYE IRIS
cut 2
brown felt

EYE LASH
cut 2 black felt

DAISY

Daisy centre

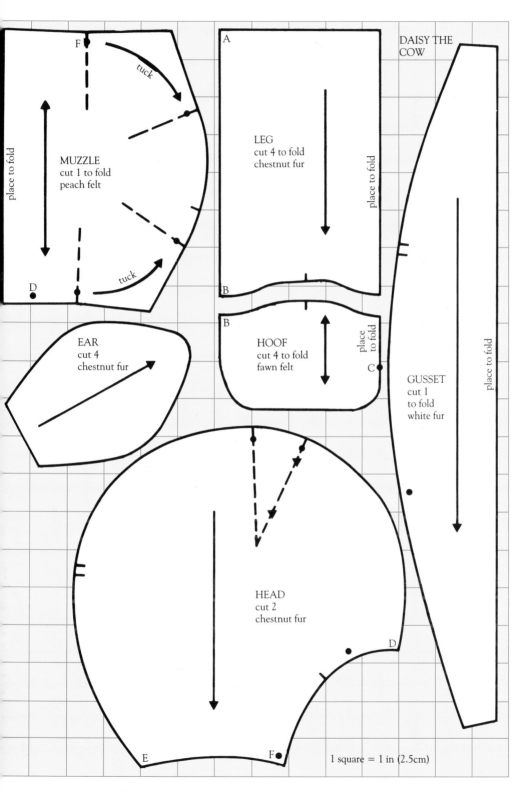

MUZZLE
cut 1 to fold
peach felt

place to fold

F

tuck

tuck

D

A

LEG
cut 4 to fold
chestnut fur

place to fold

DAISY THE
COW

B

EAR
cut 4
chestnut fur

B

HOOF
cut 4 to fold
fawn felt

place
to fold

C

GUSSET
cut 1
to fold
white fur

place to fold

HEAD
cut 2
chestnut fur

D

E

F

1 square = 1 in (2.5cm)

15

Ruff the sheepdog

Ruff the sheepdog and Felina the farmyard cat on pages 20–21 are made from the same pattern, with changes to the head shape, the ears and tail. The patterns for both animals are on pages 18–19.

Materials
12in (30cm) of 54in (137cm)-wide silver grey luxury pile fur fabric
12in (30cm) of 54in (137cm)-wide white luxury pile fur fabric
Two ½in (13.5mm) blue toy eyes
One ⅞in (23mm) black animal snout
Washable polyester toy filling

Preparation
1 Draw a pattern from the graph pattern on pages 18–19. Put in all the marks, words and numerals. Cut out the pattern pieces.

2 From the silver-grey fur, cut 1 under back on the fold, 2 tails, 1 upper back on the fold and four ears. From white fur, cut 4 paws, 1 under front on the fold and 1 upper front on the fold. From the same fur, cut 2 heads.

Making the toy
3 Stitch the tails together leaving the straight ends open. Turn right side out and stuff lightly. Baste the ends together and baste to the under back, matching points A.

4 Stitch the paws to the under back and upper back B–C. Stitch the under front to the under back and the upper front to the upper back D–E.

5 Make tiny holes at the eye positions. Stitch the heads together leaving the straight edge open. Turn right side out and attach the eyes (see page 8). Push the stalk of the snout through the seam at the nose position and fix in place.

5 Pin the straight edge of the head to the round neck edge on the upper front and back with the head facing towards one front paw. Stitch.

6 Fold the under front and back in half along the fold lines matching E. Stitch F–E–G.

7 Stitch the upper front and back to the under front and back, right sides facing, leaving an opening to turn. Turn right side out and stuff firmly. Slipstitch the opening closed.

8 Stitch the ears together in pairs, right side facing, leaving a gap to turn. Turn right side out and slip stitch the opening closed. Hand sew the top of the ears to the head.

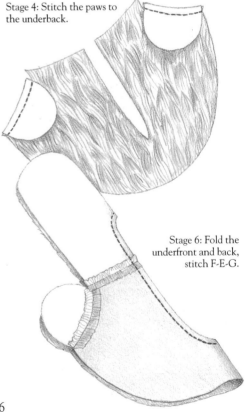

Stage 4: Stitch the paws to the underback.

Stage 6: Fold the underfront and back, stitch F-E-G.

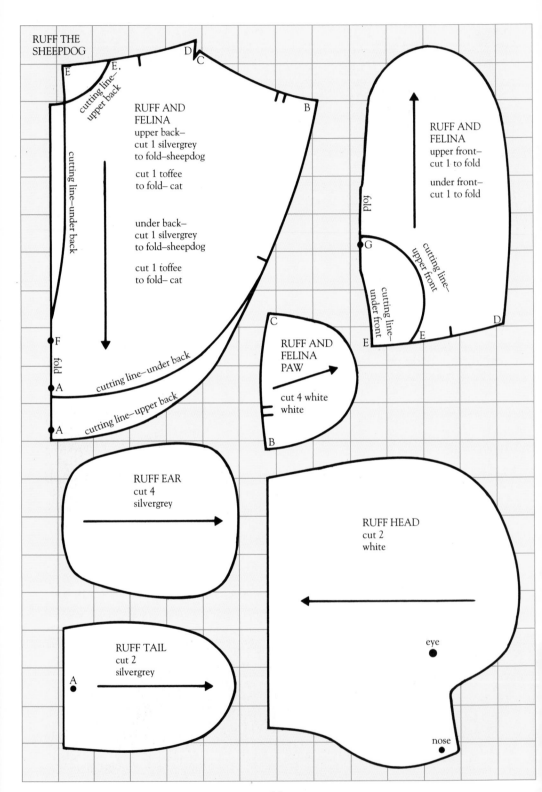

RUFF THE
SHEEPDOG

cutting line–
upper back

cutting line–under back

RUFF AND
FELINA
upper back–
cut 1 silvergrey
to fold–sheepdog

cut 1 toffee
to fold– cat

under back–
cut 1 silvergrey
to fold–sheepdog

cut 1 toffee
to fold– cat

fold

cutting line–under back

cutting line–upper back

RUFF AND
FELINA
upper front–
cut 1 to fold

under front–
cut 1 to fold

fold

cutting line–
upper front

cutting line–
under front

RUFF AND
FELINA
PAW

cut 4 white
white

RUFF EAR
cut 4
silvergrey

RUFF HEAD
cut 2
white

eye

RUFF TAIL
cut 2
silvergrey

nose

18

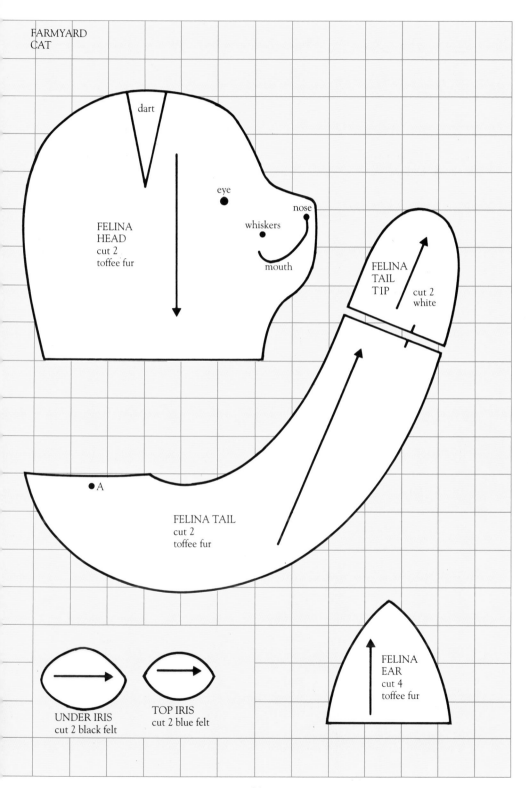

FARMYARD
CAT

dart

eye

nose

FELINA
HEAD
cut 2
toffee fur

whiskers

mouth

FELINA
TAIL
TIP
cut 2
white

•A

FELINA TAIL
cut 2
toffee fur

FELINA
EAR
cut 4
toffee fur

UNDER IRIS
cut 2 black felt

TOP IRIS
cut 2 blue felt

Felina the farmyard cat

This pretty cat would make a charming gift for a little girl
to keep on her bed.

Materials

20in (50cm) of 54in (137cm)-wide toffee
  polished fur fabric
12in (30cm) of 54in (137cm)-wide white
  polished fur fabric
Two ½in (12mm) blue toy cat eyes
⅝in (15mm) pink cat nose
Scraps of blue and black felt
1⅛yd (1m) of 1in (2.5cm)-wide turquoise
  satin ribbon
Ginger-coloured stranded embroidery thread
White toy-making whiskers
Washable polyester toy filling

Preparation

1 Draw a pattern from the graph pattern on
pages 18–19 and adapt the pattern as
instructed for the cat's head, ears and tail.

2 From toffee fur, cut out 1 under back to
the fold, 2 tails and 1 upper back to the fold.
From white fur, cut out 2 tail tips. Cut 2
heads and 4 ears.

3 From white fur cut 4 paws, 1 under front
on the fold and 1 upper front on the fold.

4 Cut 2 top irises from blue felt. Cut 2
under irises from black felt.

Making the toy

5 Stitch the tail tips to the tail then stitch
the complete tails together, leaving the
straight end open. Turn right side out and
stuff lightly. Baste the ends together and
baste to the under back matching points A.

6 Stitch the paws to the under back and
upper back B–C. Stitch the under front to
the under back and the upper front to the
upper back D–E.

7 Make tiny holes at the eye positions on
the heads and through the blue iris, then the
black iris. Fix in position. Stitch the darts.

8 Stitch the heads together leaving the
straight edge open. Turn right side out. Push
the stalk of the nose through the seam at the
nose position and fix in place.

9 Pin the straight edge of the head to the
round neck edge on the upper front and
back, easing the front and back to fit and
with the head facing towards one front paw,
stitch.

10 Fold the under front and back in half
along the fold lines matching point E. Stitch
F–E–G.

11 Stitch the upper front and back to the
under front and back leaving an opening to
turn. Turn right side out and stuff firmly.
Slipstitch the opening closed.

12 Stitch the ears together in pairs leaving
an opening to turn. Turn right side out
slipstitch the openings closed and hand sew
to the head.

13 Embroider the mouth in stem stitch
using 3 strands of pink embroidery thread.
Attach the whiskers to the face (see page 8).

Porky the pig

Always a favourite farmyard toy, this little pig is one that will be much loved by small children. The tail is made of pink felt but for a very small child, it might be better to plait a tail and sew it to the body.

Materials

8in (20cm) of 60in (150cm)-wide peach-coloured close-pile fur fabric
9in (23cm) square of peach felt
Two ⅜in (9mm) black toy eyes
Black stranded embroidery thread
Washable polyester toy filling

Preparation

1 Draw a pattern from the graph pattern and put in all marks, words and numerals. Cut out pattern pieces.
From the fur fabric, cut out 2 bodies, 2 undersides, 1 head gusset, 1 snout and 4 ears.
Cut 4 felt hooves.

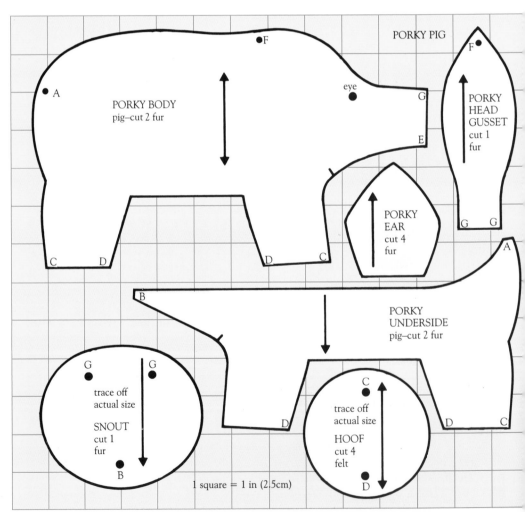

PORKY PIG

PORKY BODY
pig–cut 2 fur

eye

PORKY HEAD GUSSET
cut 1 fur

PORKY EAR
cut 4 fur

PORKY UNDERSIDE
pig–cut 2 fur

trace off actual size

SNOUT
cut 1 fur

trace off actual size

HOOF
cut 4 felt

1 square = 1 in (2.5cm)

2 Make tiny holes on the bodies at the eye positions. Stitch the undersides together A–B leaving a 3¼in (8cm) gap in the middle. Stitch the undersides to the bodies A–C, D–D and C–E.

3 Stitch the bodies together A–F and then the head gusset between the bodies G–F–G. Sew the snout to the pig matching B and G and easing the snout to fit.

4 Sew the hooves to the pig matching C and D. Turn right side out and attach the eyes. Stuff the pig firmly and slipstitch the opening closed.

5 Stitch the ears together in pairs leaving the lower, straight edges open. Turn right side out and turn under ¼in (6mm) on the lower edges. Slipstitch the lower edges together and hand sew to the top of the head.

6 Work two French knots for nostrils on the snout using doubled embroidery thread.

7 Cut a strip of pink felt for a tail and gather up to curl it. Sew to the pig at the back. Alternatively, plait 9 lengths of embroidery thread together in threes and sew firmly to the pig's body. Knot the thread ends.

Dottie the duck

This charming little toy is small enough for a very little child but older children will find it just as lovable. The fabric quantities are not great so this a good project for fund-raising – toys always sell well.

Materials

12in (30cm) of 60in (150cm)-wide white
  polished fur fabric
6in (15cm) square of yellow cotton jersey
Two ⅜in (9mm) black toy eyes
Washable polyester toy filling

Preparation

1 Draw a pattern from the graph pattern and put in all marks, words and numerals. Cut out pattern pieces.

2 From the fur fabric, cut 2 duck shapes on the fold, 4 wings and 1 base piece on the fold. From the yellow jersey, cut out 2 beaks and 4 feet.

Making the toy

3 Stitch the darts on the duck shapes. Mark the position of the broken line with a row of basting. On one duck piece, make tiny holes at the eye position (this will be the front). Fix the eyes in place.

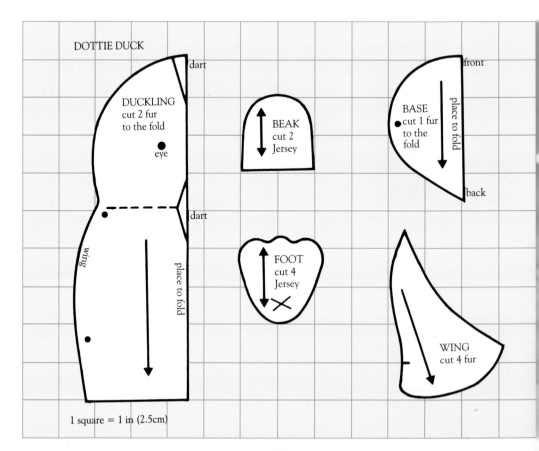

DOTTIE DUCK

DUCKLING
cut 2 fur
to the fold

eye

dart

wing

place to fold

dart

BEAK
cut 2
Jersey

FOOT
cut 4
Jersey

front

BASE
cut 1 fur
to the
fold

place to fold

back

WING
cut 4 fur

1 square = 1 in (2.5cm)

4 Stitch the wings together in pairs along the notched edges. Turn right side out and baste the raw edges together. Baste the wings to the front between the dots. Stitch the duck shapes together leaving the lower, straight edges open and with a 3½in (9cm) gap to turn.

5 Stitch the base to the duck, matching the fold lines and dots to the seams. Turn right side out and stuff. Slipstitch the opening closed. Gather along the basted line (refer to the pattern) to define the head.

6 Stitch the beaks together leaving the straight ends open. Turn right side out and turn ¼in (6mm) on the straight edge to the inside. Stuff the beak then pin to the face. Hand sew in place along the turned-in edges, using slip stitches or hemming.

7 Stitch the feet together in pairs, wrong sides facing. Cut the cross (see pattern) on one layer of jersey on each foot and turn right side out. Stuff the feet fairly firmly and oversew the cut edges together. Sew the feet under the base.

25

Lamb muff

*Just the thing to keep the hands warm on a cold and frosty day – and
such fun to carry around. The lamb's head purse is detachable.*

Materials
½yd (40cm) of 54in (137cm)-wide cream
  curly fur
¼yd (20cm) of 54in (137cm)-wide black
  curly fur
½yd (40cm) of 36in (90cm)-wide cream
  lining
9in (23cm) square of black felt
½yd (40cm) of medium-weight wadding
12in (30cm) square of black lining
Two ⅜in (1cm) blue toy eyes
Three Velcro spot-ons
1¼yds (120cm) green cord
Washable polyester toy filling

Preparation
1 From the cream fur, cut out a rectangle
13½ × 12½in (34 × 32cm) for the muff and a
piece of wadding 13½ × 10¼in (34 × 26cm).
Tack the wadding to the wrong side of the
muff 1⅛in (3cm) in from the ends.

2 From the black fur, cut out 4 rectangles
for the legs 3½ × 3in (9 × 7.5cm) and from
black felt, cut out 4 rectangles for the hooves
3 × 1⅝in (7.5 × 4cm). Stitch each leg to a
hoof then fold lengthways in half and stitch
the long edge and across the end of the hoof.

Making the muff
3 Turn legs right side out and stuff lightly.
Tack across the upper edges. Tack 2 legs to
the right side of the muff on one short edge
1⅝in (4cm) in from the ends and the
remaining legs ¼in (6mm) in from first legs.

4 From the cream lining, cut out a rectangle
13½ × 8¼in (34 × 21cm). Stitch to the muff
along the long edges and turn right side out.
Fold the muff in half with the fur sides
together and stitch the raw edges of the fur
together, extending the stitching into the
lining. Slipstitch remaining edges of lining
together then turn fur to the outside.

5 Thread the cord through the muff. Place
the ends side by side and bind tightly
together with thread. Hand sew the join
inside the muff.

Making the lamb's head purse
6 To make the purse, trace the head shape
and cut out 1 face to the fold and 4 ears in
black fur, 1 face in felt and 2 faces to the fold
in black lining. Fix the eyes in place on the
fur face then stitch each lining to a fur and
felt face, leaving an opening to turn.

7 Turn right side out and slipstitch the
openings closed. Pin the faces together with
the linings facing. Fasten together with a
Velcro spot-on between the dots on the
upper edge then hand sew together around
the outer edges between the dots.

8 Stitch the ears together in pairs, leaving
an opening to turn. Turn right side out and
sew to the purse at the dots. Attach the
purse to the muff with two Velcro spot-ons.

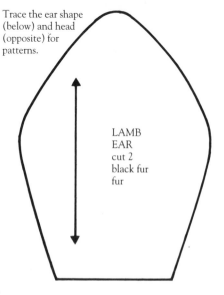

Trace the ear shape
(below) and head
(opposite) for
patterns.

LAMB
EAR
cut 2
black fur
fur

trace off actual size

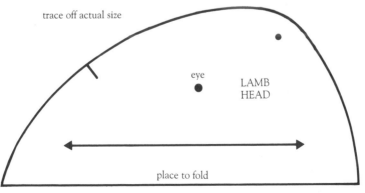

eye

LAMB
HEAD

place to fold

27

TWO

Country Folk

Wily old fox

This pattern introduces you to jointed toys, which are not difficult to make. Toy joints can be obtained from specialist craft shops and some addresses are given on page 96.

Materials
28in (70cm) of 60in (150cm)-wide chestnut polished fur fabric
20in (50cm) of 60in (150cm)-wide white polished fur fabric
16in (40cm) of 54in (137cm)-wide chestnut long hair fur fabric
8in (2ocm) of 60in (150cm)-wide oatmeal-coloured close pile fur fabric
8in (20cm) of 54in (137cm)-wide white long hair fur fabric
Scrap of dark brown felt
Two ½in (12mm) amber toy eyes
⅞in (23mm) black animal snout
Four 1¼in (3.5cm) toy joints
Black toy whiskers
Washable polyester toy filling

Preparation
1 Draw a pattern from the graph patterns on pages 32–33, 34–35 on squared paper. Put in all marks, words and numerals. Cut out the pattern pieces.

2 From the chestnut fur, cut 1 back gusset on the fold, 4 arms and 4 legs. Cut 2 ears from the same fur. From the long-haired chestnut fur, cut 2 tails on the fold.

3 From the white fur, cut 1 front gusset on the fold. From the long-haired white fur, cut 2 tail tips. From the close pile fur, cut 2 soles and 2 ears. Cut 2 irises in dark brown felt.

Making the toy
4 Make tiny holes on the bodies and front gusset at the joint, eyes and nose positions. Stitch the gussets together A–A and B–B. Stitch the gussets between the bodies A–C–B–D–A, leaving a gap to turn. Turn right side out.

5 Pierce a hole through the centre of the irises. Fix the eyes and nose in place (refer to page 8).

6 Make a tiny hole at the joint position on a pair of arms and legs. Stitch each 'joint' arm to a plain one leaving a gap to turn. Turn right side out. From the inside, insert the stalk of a joint through the hole. Stuff the arms and slipstitch the opening closed.

7 Stitch each 'joint' leg to a plain one leaving the lower, straight edge open between E and F and a gap at the back of the leg for stuffing.

8 Stitch the soles to the legs matching E and F. Turn right side out and from the inside, insert the stalk of a joint through each hole. Stuff the legs and slipstitch the openings closed. Insert the joint stalks of the arms and legs through the holes on the body with the limbs facing forward. Fix on the washers to secure the arms and legs in place.

9 Stuff the body and slipstitch the opening closed. Stitch a close pile ear to a polished fur ear leaving the lower, straight edge open. Turn right side out and turn under ¼in (6mm) on the lower edge. Fold in half in a 'V' shape and hand sew the ears to the top of the head with the close pile fur facing the front.

10 Stitch the tail tips to the tails G–G. Stitch the complete tails together leaving the straight end open. Turn right side out and stuff lightly. Turn under ¼in (6mm) on the lower edges and hand sew the tail to the back of the fox. Attach the whiskers to the head (see page 9 for the technique).

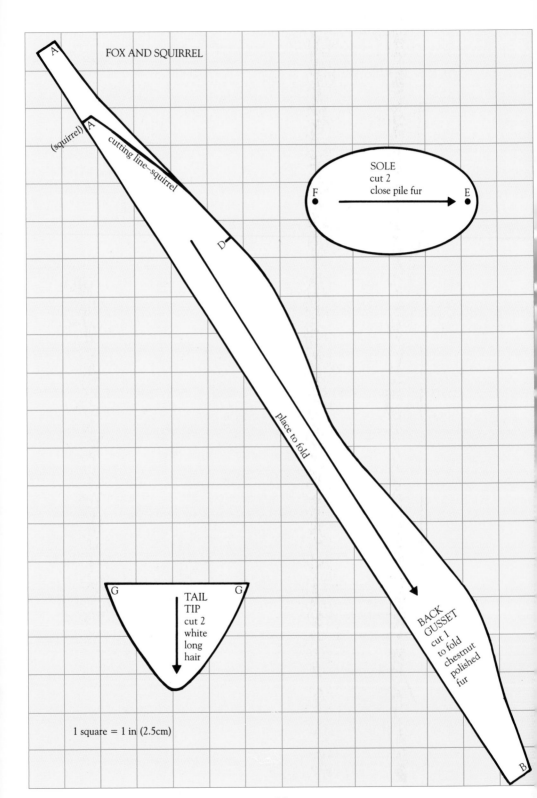

FOX AND SQUIRREL

A

(squirrel) A

cutting line–squirrel

D

place to fold

SOLE
cut 2
close pile fur

F ● ——————————→ ● E

G · · · · · · · · · · · · · G
TAIL
TIP
cut 2
white
long
hair
↓

BACK
GUSSET
cut 1
to fold
chestnut
polished
fur

B

1 square = 1 in (2.5cm)

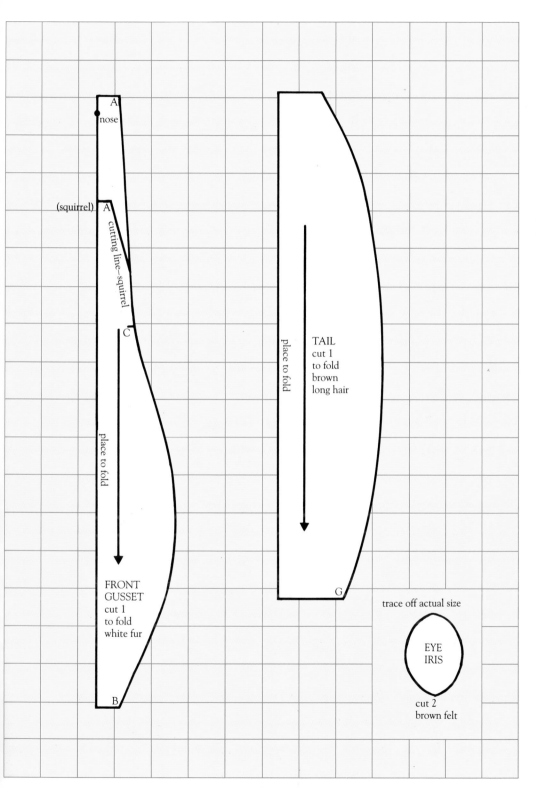

A
nose

(squirrel) A
cutting line—squirrel
C

place to fold

FRONT
GUSSET
cut 1
to fold
white fur

B

place to fold

TAIL
cut 1
to fold
brown
long hair

G

trace off actual size

EYE
IRIS

cut 2
brown felt

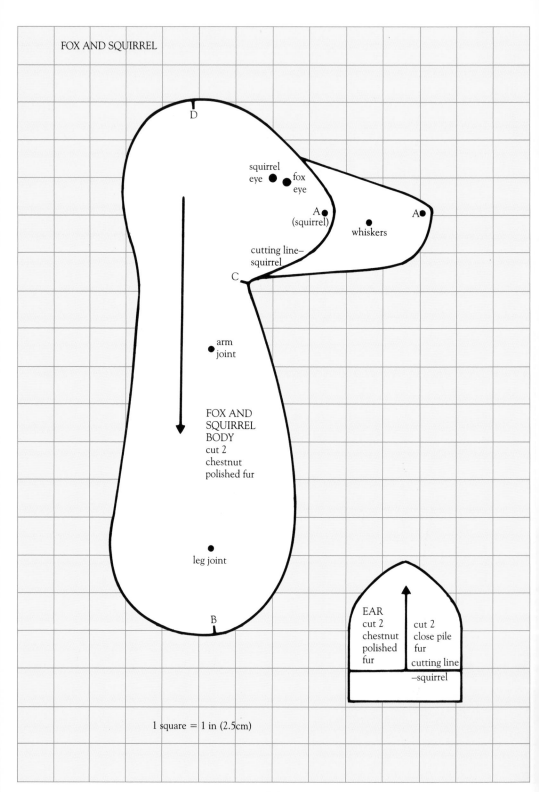

FOX AND SQUIRREL

D

squirrel
eye ● ● fox
eye

A●
(squirrel)
● whiskers
A●

cutting line–
squirrel

C

● arm
joint

FOX AND
SQUIRREL
BODY
cut 2
chestnut
polished fur

● leg joint

B

EAR
cut 2
chestnut
polished
fur

cut 2
close pile
fur
cutting line
–squirrel

1 square = 1 in (2.5cm)

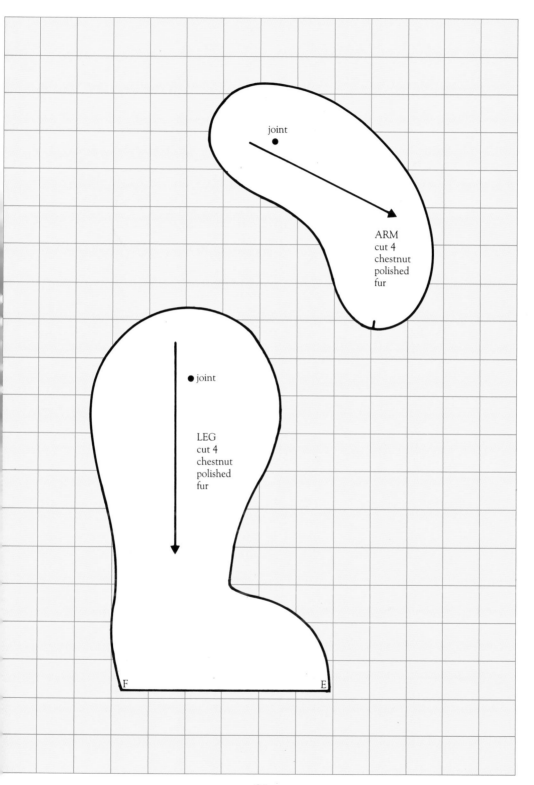

joint
•

ARM
cut 4
chestnut
polished
fur

• joint

LEG
cut 4
chestnut
polished
fur

F

E

Grey squirrel

This toy is made from the same basic pattern as the fox, with adaptations to the head, ears and tail. If you prefer, the front of the squirrel could be made in white fur.

Materials

28in (70cm) of 60in (150cm)-wide silver-fox polished fur fabric
28in (70cm) of 54in (137cm)-wide silver-fox luxury pile fur fabric
Scrap of dark brown felt
Two ½in (12mm) amber toy eyes
⅞in (23mm) black animal snout
Four 1¼in (3.5cm) toy joints
Washable polyester toy filling

Preparation

1 Draw a pattern from the graph patterns on pages 32–33, 34–35 adapting the pattern as instructed for the squirrel's head, ears and tail.

2 Cut out the pattern pieces.

3 From the grey fur, cut out 2 bodies, 1 back gusset on the fold, 1 front gusset on the fold. From the same fur, cut 4 arms, 4 legs, 2 soles and 2 ears.

4 Cut 2 tails and 2 ears from the luxury pile fabric. Cut 2 irises from brown felt.

Making the toy

5 Make holes on the bodies and front gusset at the joint, eye and nose positions. Stitch the gussets together A–A and B–B. Stitch the gussets between the bodies A–C–B–D–A, leaving a gap to turn. Turn right side out.

6 Pierce a hole through the centres of the felt irises. Insert the stalk of the eyes through the hole, then fix to the bodies. Fix the snout to the front gusset.

7 Make a tiny hole at the joint position on a pair of arms and legs. Stitch each 'joint' arm to a plain one leaving a gap to turn. Turn right side out and from the inside, insert the stalk of a joint through the hole. Stuff the arms and slipstitch the openings closed.

8 Stitch each 'joint' leg to a plain one leaving the lower, straight edges open between E and F and a gap at the back of the leg for stuffing.

9 Stitch the soles to the legs matching E and F. Turn right side out and from the inside, insert the stalk of a joint through each hole. Stuff the legs and slipstitch the openings closed. Insert the joint stalks of the arms and legs through the holes on the body with the limbs facing forward. Fix on the washers to secure the arms and legs in place.

10 Stuff the body and slipstitch the opening closed. Stitch each polished fur ear to a luxury pile fur ear leaving the lower, straight edge open. Turn right side out and turn under ¼in (6mm) on the lower edge. Slipstitch the lower edges together. Hand sew the ears to the top of the head with the polished fur facing the front.

11 Stitch the tails together leaving an opening to turn. Turn right side out and stuff lightly. Slipstitch the opening closed. Hand sew the wide end of the tail to the back of the squirrel close to the base. Pin the tail approximately 9in (23cm) below the tip to the back of the squirrel between the top of the arms. Hand sew in position and bend the tip over backwards.

Wise owls

There's nothing like a pair of owls to keep a little girl's ears warm on chilly days! These charming little toys could be made without the hair band as stocking filler gifts for young children.

Materials

8in (20cm) of 54in (137cm)-wide sand-coloured beaver fur fabric
8in (20cm) of 60in (150cm)-wide cream polished fur fabric
16in (40cm) of 36in (90cm)-wide green cotton fabric
8in (20cm) of medium-weight wadding
9in (23cm) square of beige felt
Four ⅝in (15mm) amber toy eyes
Plastic or metal hair band
Washable polyester toy filling

Preparation

1 Draw a pattern from the graph pattern on squared paper and put in all marks, words and numerals. Cut out the pattern pieces.

2 From the sand-coloured fur cut 4 owl shapes. From the cream-coloured fur cut 8 eye patches and 4 wings.

3 From the beige felt, cut 4 beaks and 4 sets of claws.

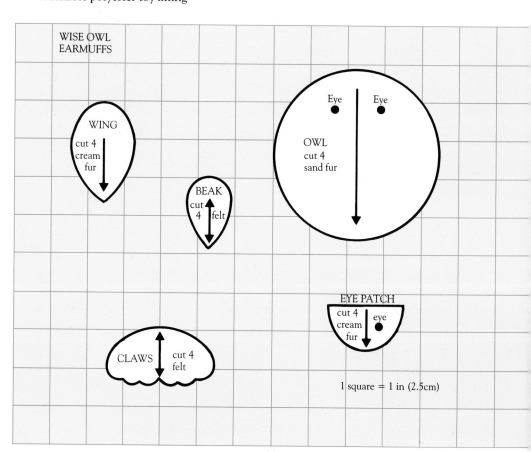

WISE OWL EARMUFFS

WING
cut 4
cream
fur

BEAK
cut 4 felt

OWL
cut 4
sand fur

Eye   Eye

EYE PATCH
cut 4
cream
fur
eye

CLAWS   cut 4
felt

1 square = 1 in (2.5cm)

Making the earmuffs

4 Wrap a length of wadding around the hairband and hand sew the edges together. Cut a bias strip of green fabric to cover the hair band. Press under ¼in (6mm) on one long edge. Wrap around the hair band pinning the pressed edge over the long raw edge. Slipstitch the pressed edge in place.

5 Make tiny holes on 2 owls at the eye positions. Stitch each plain owl to one with eye holes leaving a gap at the top. Turn right side out.

6 Make tiny holes on 2 pairs of eye patches at the eye positions. Stitch each plain patch

to one with eye holes along the straight edges. Insert the stalk of the eyes through the holes in the patches and fix through the holes on the owls.

7 Stuff the owls and insert the ends of the hair band inside. slipstitch the openings closed, sewing the owls securely to the hair band. Pin the wings to the sides of the owls and hand sew in position at the top edge.

8 Stitch the beaks and claws together in pairs leaving an opening to turn. Turn right side out and stuff. Slipstitch the openings closed. Hand sew the beaks to the owls' faces and the claws underneath the bases.

Brock the badger

Badgers – one of Britain's protected species – are great favourites with young and old alike. Although children will adore this cosy little creature, it could also make a wonderful toy for fund-raising.

Materials

16in (40cm) of 54in (137cm)-wide black wild animal fur
8in (20cm) of 54in (137cm)-wide white wild animal fur
Scrap of brown felt
Scrap of black felt
Two ½in (12mm) amber toy eyes
Washable polyester toy filling

Preparation

1 Draw a pattern from the graph pattern on pages 42–43 on squared paper. Put in all marks, words and numerals. Cut out the pattern pieces.

2 From the black fur, cut 2 upper heads. From the same fabric cut 1 body on the fold, 1 base on the fold, 2 tails and 4 ears. From white fur, cut 1 head gusset on the fold and 2 lower heads. Cut a nose from black felt and 2 irises from brown felt.

3 Make tiny holes on the upper heads at the eye positions. Stitch the upper heads to the lower heads A–B. Stitch the lower heads together C–D.

4 Stitch the head gusset between the heads E–C–E. Pierce a hole through the centre of the irises. Insert the stalk of the eye through the holes and fix in position on the upper heads.

5 Fold the body in half and stitch the centre front seam D–F and the centre back seam G–H. Stitch the head to the body matching B–D–B.

6 Stitch the tails together leaving the lower, straight end open. Turn right side out and tack the end to the base matching G.

Stitch the body to the base matching F and G and leaving a gap to turn. Turn right side out and stuff firmly. Slipstitch the opening closed.

7 Stitch the ears together in pairs leaving the lower, straight ends open. Turn right side out and turn under ¼in (6mm) on the lower edges. Slipstitch the lower edges together and hand sew to the top of the head.

8 Hand sew the nose to the badger's face at C (refer to pattern on pages 42–43).

Stage 4: Stitch the head gusset between the heads.

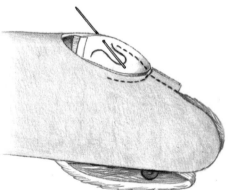

Stage 5: Stitch the head to the body.

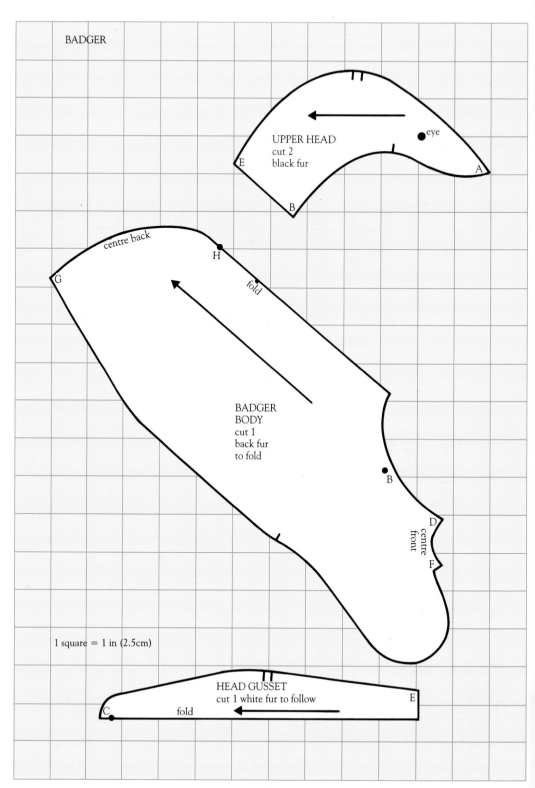

BADGER

UPPER HEAD
cut 2
black fur

eye

E

A

B

centre back

H

fold

G

BADGER
BODY
cut 1
back fur
to fold

B

D

centre
front

F

1 square = 1 in (2.5cm)

HEAD GUSSET
cut 1 white fur to follow

E

C

fold

42

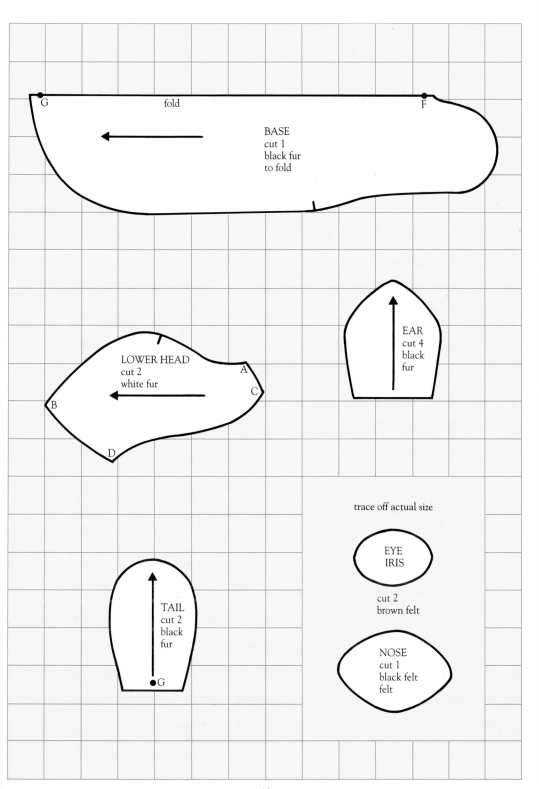

G   fold   F

BASE
cut 1
black fur
to fold

EAR
cut 4
black
fur

LOWER HEAD
cut 2
white fur

A
C
B
D

trace off actual size

EYE
IRIS

cut 2
brown felt

TAIL
cut 2
black
fur

G

NOSE
cut 1
black felt
felt

G

THREE

Jungle Friends

Tiger bright

What a lot of fun you are going to have with this tiger hand-puppet! The 'tigery' face is achieved by using tiger-striped fur – look for this fabric when you are planning the puppet – there really is no substitute.

Materials

12in (30cm) of 54in (137cm)-wide tiger-striped fur fabric
8in (20cm) of 60in (150cmm)-wide oatmeal close pile fur fabric
8in (20cm) of 54in (137cm)-wide white wild animal fur fabric
12in (30cm) of 36in (90cm)-wide lining fabric
6in (15cm) square of black felt
Two ½in (12mm) amber toy eyes
Washable polyester toy filling

Preparation

1 Draw a pattern from the graph pattern on pages 48–49, on squared paper. Put in all marks, words and numerals. Cut out the pattern pieces.

2 From the striped fur fabric, cut 2 bodies on the fold, 2 upper faces, 2 back heads and 2 ears. Cut also a strip 9 × 2½in (22 × 6cm) for the tail.

3 From the white fur fabric, cut 2 lower faces. From the close pile fur fabric, cut 1 muzzle and 2 ears.

4 From the lining, cut 2 bodies on the fold. From felt, cut 2 irises, 1 nose and mouth.

Stage 8: Stitch the upper faces together.

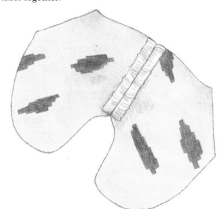

IRIS
cut 2
black felt

trace off actual size

NOSE AND MOUTH
cut 1 black felt

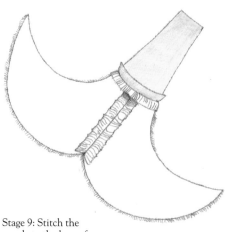

Stage 9: Stitch the muzzle to the lower faces.

Making the toy

5 Fold the tail lengthways in half and stitch the long edges together and across the lower end. Turn right side out and baste to the lower edge of one body piece at the centre. (This will be the back.)

6 Stitch the lining bodies together B–A–A–B and turn right side out. Stitch the fur bodies together A–B, slip the lining inside the fur body and stitch together around the lower edges matching points B and leaving a 4in (10cm) opening. Turn and slipstitch the opening closed.

47

7 Slip your hand inside the body and pin the fur and lining together at the 'neck' matching A and C. Hand sew the raw edge of the fur to the lining.

8 Make tiny holes at the eye positions on the upper faces then stitch the upper faces together D–E. Stitch the back heads together C–D. Stitch the darts.

9 Stitch the lower faces together C–F. Stitch the muzzle to the lower faces G–F–G.

10 Stitch the lower faces and muzzle to the upper face H–G–E–G–H, hand sewing the G–E–G part of the seam. Stitch each tiger-striped ear to a close pile ear around the notched edges. Turn right side out and baste the raw edges together.

11 Baste the ears to the top of the upper faces 2½in (6cm) apart, with the close pile fur ears facing the face. Stitch the back head to the face A–H–D–H–A. Turn right side out.

12 Make tiny holes in the centre of the irises. Insert the stalk of the eyes through the holes then fix in position to the upper face.

13 Stuff the head around the outer edges, place the end of a wide pen or paintbrush handle inside centrally and continue stuffing firmly. Remove the pen and turn under ¼in (6mm) on the lower edges.

14 Slip your hand into the body and insert a finger in the top of the lining. Place the head on top facing forward and pin the turned under edge ¼in (6mm) below the raw fur edge, matching A and C. Hand sew in place.

15 Pin the nose and mouth to the face with the top edge level with the lower edge of the muzzle. Hand sew in place.

> Although toys can be given button eyes or eyes cut from felt, it is always better to use proper safety eyes.

Stage 10: Stitch the lower faces and muzzle to the upper face.

Stage 12: Push the eye stalk through felt, then through the face.

Stage 14: Slip your hand into the body, with forefinger in the lining.

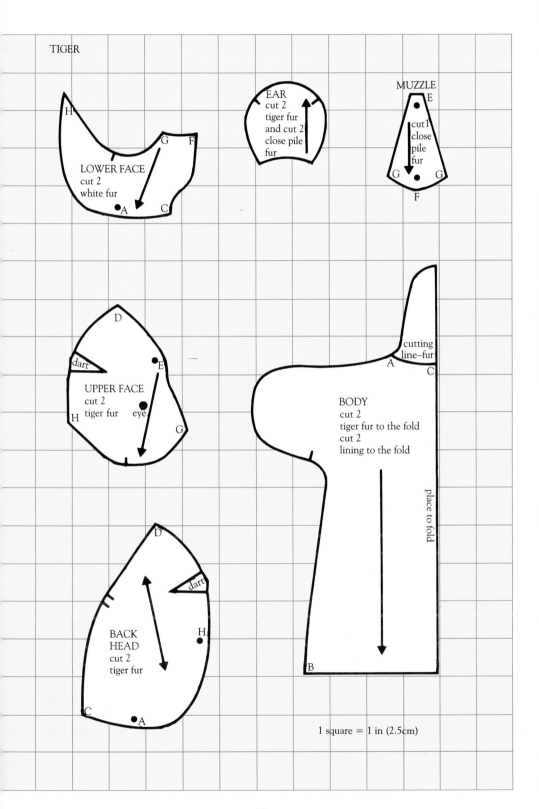

TIGER

EAR
cut 2
tiger fur
and cut 2
close pile
fur

MUZZLE
cut 1
close
pile
fur

H

G F

LOWER FACE
cut 2
white fur

A C

D

dart

E

UPPER FACE
cut 2
tiger fur   eye

H

G

cutting
line–fur

A

C

BODY
cut 2
tiger fur to the fold
cut 2
lining to the fold

place to fold

D

dart

BACK
HEAD
cut 2
tiger fur

H

C

A

B

1 square = 1 in (2.5cm)

49

Cheeky monkey

This happy-looking fellow is one of the biggest toys in the book, but you will find it is very simple to make. Think of the pleasure you are going to give to some lucky child!

Materials

20in (50cm) of 54in (137cm)-wide chestnut long hair fur fabric
16in (40cm) of 60in (150cm)-wide peach-coloured felt
Scrap of chestnut-coloured felt
Two ⅜in (9mm) black toy eyes
Chestnut stranded embroidery thread
Washable polyester toy filling

Preparation

1 Draw a pattern from the diagram on this page. Put in all marks, words and numerals. Cut out the pattern pieces.

2 From fur fabric, cut out 2 shapes. Cut out the face circle once (front). Mark the position of the broken lines with a line of basting stitches.

3 Cut 2 rectangles 10 × 7½in (25 × 19cm) for the legs, 2 rectangles 8⅝ × 6in (22 × 15cm) for the arms, and a strip 17 × 2¾in (43 × 7cm) for the tail. All pieces should be cut with the pile running parallel with the long edges.

4 Draw a pattern from the graph pattern on page 52. Put in all marks, words and numerals. Use the patterns to cut pieces as follows: from peach felt, cut 4 hands. 1 upper face on the fold, 2 muzzles on the fold, 4 ears and 4 feet. Trace the shape and, from chestnut felt, cut 1 nose.

Making the toy

5 Fold the legs and arms lengthways in half, right sides facing and stitch along the long edges. Turn the legs right side out and tack to the lower edge of the front body, ⅜in (1cm) in from the long edges.

6 Fold the tail lengthways in half and stitch along the long edges and across the lower edge. Turn right side out and tack to the body between the legs.

7 Stitch hands together in pairs leaving the straight ends open and stuff with a thin layer of toy filling. Baste across the straight ends then stitch along the broken lines to form the fingers.

Draw the basic body from this diagram.

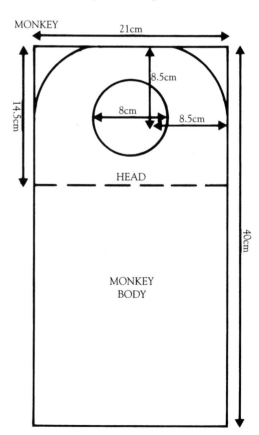

MONKEY

21cm

14.5cm

8.5cm

8cm

8.5cm

HEAD

40cm

MONKEY BODY

9 Gather around the end of each arm and insert a hand inside with the raw edges level. Pull up the gathers to fit the hand then stitch across the raw edges. Turn right side out and stuff lightly so the arms bend easily. Baste across the raw edges then baste to the front body ¾in (2cm) below the broken line with the thumbs upwards.

10 Make tiny holes at the eye positions on the upper face. Stitch the darts in the muzzles and snip the seam allowance to the dart points. Stitch the muzzle together along the notched edges.

11 Stitch the muzzle to the upper face matching fold lines and easing the muzzle to fit. Stitch the face to the face circle with fold lines matching the centre of the monkey head and with the upper face at the top.

12 Stitch the ears together in pairs leaving the inner curves open. Turn right side out and stuff lightly. Baste across the raw edges. Baste the ears to the front monkey shape 2½in (6.5cm) above the broken line.

13 Now stitch the monkey shapes together leaving a 7¼in (18cm) opening on the lower edge. Turn right side out and fix the eyes to the upper face. Stuff the monkey lightly so that it has a soft, squashy feel. Gather along the broken line slightly to define the head. Slipstitch the opening closed.

14 Draw the marked circle on the right side of one pair of feet and cut a slit within the circles to turn right side out. Stitch the feet

together in pairs. Turn right side out and stuff lightly.

15 Lightly stuff the legs and turn under ¼in (6mm) on the lower edges. Hand sew the lower folded leg edges to the circle on the feet with the 'big toes' inwards.

16 Sew the nose to the muzzle, covering the end of the top dart. Embroider the mouth in stem stitch using 3 strands of embroidery thread and stitching along the muzzle seam.

Stage 11: Stitch the muzzle to the upper face.

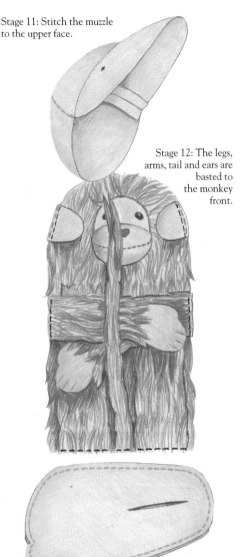

Stage 12: The legs, arms, tail and ears are basted to the monkey front.

Stage 8: Stitch along the felt hands to form fingers.

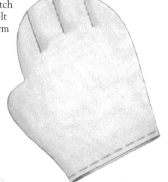

Stage 14: Stitched feet together, turn to right side through the slit.

MONKEY

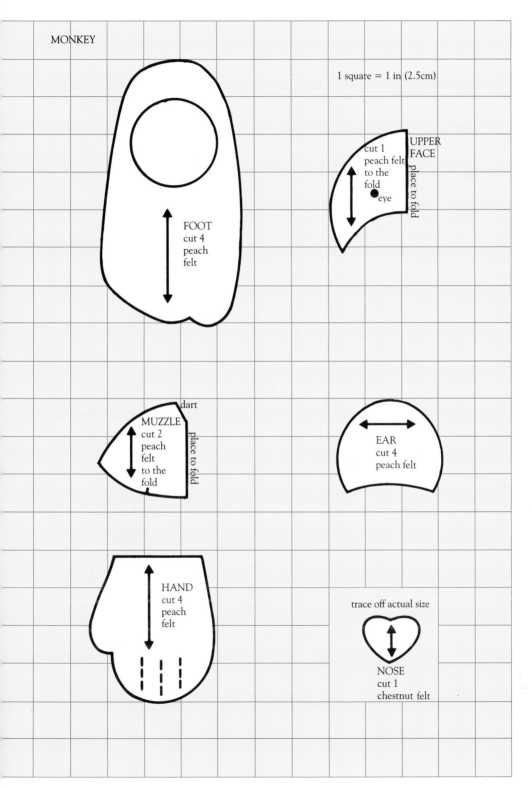

1 square = 1 in (2.5cm)

FOOT
cut 4
peach
felt

UPPER
FACE
cut 1
peach felt
to the
fold
place to fold
● eye

MUZZLE
cut 2
peach
felt
to the
fold
dart
place to fold

EAR
cut 4
peach felt

HAND
cut 4
peach
felt

trace off actual size

NOSE
cut 1
chestnut felt

53

Beanbag lion

Beanbag toys will take a lot of rough handling as long as the seams are properly stitched. Do not attempt to hand sew this type of toy – or you could find the filling seeping out after a particularly strenuous game.

Materials
20in (50cm) of 56in (140cm)-wide ochre-coloured cotton fabric
8in (20cm) of 54in (137cm)-wide honey-coloured long haired fur fabric
Polystyrene granules
Black fabric paint

Baste the legs and arms to one body piece. The ear shape diagram is below. Trace the face from the pattern (below right).

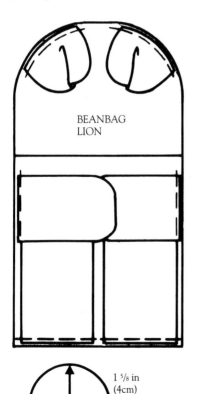

BEANBAG
LION

1 ⁵/₈ in (4cm)

EAR

1 ³/₈ in (3.5cm)

Preparation
1 From the ochre fabric cut 2 rectangles 13½ × 7¼in (34 × 18.5cm) for the body. Cut 4 semi-circles with a 1⅝in (4cm) radius for the ears and add 1⅜in (3.5cm) on the straight edges. Cut 2 rectangles 6¾in × 5¼in (17 × 13.5cm) for the legs and 2 rectangles 5½ × 4¼in (14 × 11cm) for the arms. Cut a strip 8 × 1¼in (20 × 4.5cm) for the tail.

2 From the fur fabric, cut a rectangle 2 × 1¼in (5 × 3cm) for the tail tip and another strip 23½ × 2¾in (60 × 7cm) for the mane, making sure the pile runs down parallel with the short ends.

Making the toy
3 Round off the centre of one short edge of both body pieces using a 6in (15cm) saucer. Draw a pencil line on the right side 8in (20cm) above the short, straight edges. Trace the features from the pattern outline and transfer centrally just above the line. Paint the face (see picture). Follow the manufacturer's instructions to make the paint permanent.

BEANBAG LION
trace off actual size

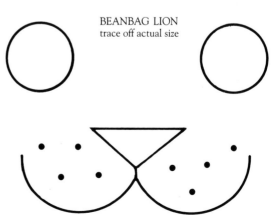

4 Stitch the ears together in pairs, leaving the straight ends open. Turn right side out and baste across the ends. Baste the ears to the top of one body piece 2in (5cm) apart.

5 Fold the legs and arms in half widthways. Curve the corners on one short end. Stitch the legs and arms along the long and curved edges. Turn to the right side and fill loosely with the polystyrene granules. Baste across the opening edges.

6 Baste the legs to the short end of one body piece, ¼in (6mm) in from the long edges, and the arms to the long edges, 4⅜in (11cm) above the short, straight end. Fold the tail lengthways in half and stitch along the length. Turn right side out with a bodkin.

7 Fold the tail tip widthways in half and stitch along the length. Insert the tail through the tail tip. Pin the top of the tail tip level with the bottom of the tail and stitch across the end through all the thicknesses. Pull the tail tip downward to the right side. Baste it between the legs.

8 Stitch the bodies together leaving an opening at the bottom. Turn right side out, fill with granules. Gather along the pencilled line and pull up to form the neck. Slipstitch the opening closed. Stitch the mane ends together, sew in a circle around the face with the pile away from the face. Turn under the raw edge, slipstitch to the seam enclosing the allowance.

Dinosaur

*Little boys, in particular, love monsters and this jointed
one will delight any child. Here the toy is made in a bright red fabric
with mauve trim but you could choose a greenish fabric with a print if
you prefer a toy with a more authentic look.*

Materials

24in (60cm) of 56in (140cm)-wide red
   glazed cotton
8in (20cm) of 56in (140cm)-wide grey-
   mauve glazed cotton
Two ¼in (6mm) black toy eyes
Four 1¼in (3.5cm) toy joints
Washable polyester toy filling

Preparation

1 Draw a pattern from the graph patterns on
pages 58, 59 and 60. Put in all marks, words
and numerals. Cut out the pattern pieces.

2 From the red fabric, cut 2 bodies, 1 gusset
to the fold, 8 legs and 4 feet pads.

3 From the grey-mauve fabric, cut 2 head
spines, 4 small spines, 6 medium spines, 6
large spines and 4 spikes.

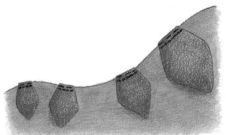

Stage 5: Baste and stitch spines
to one body piece.

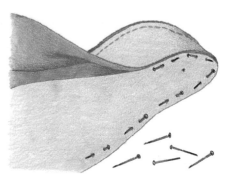

Stage 7: Pin, then baste the gusset to the body.

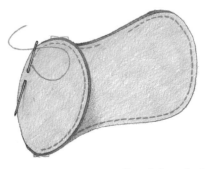

Stage 8: Baste the foot pad
to the leg.

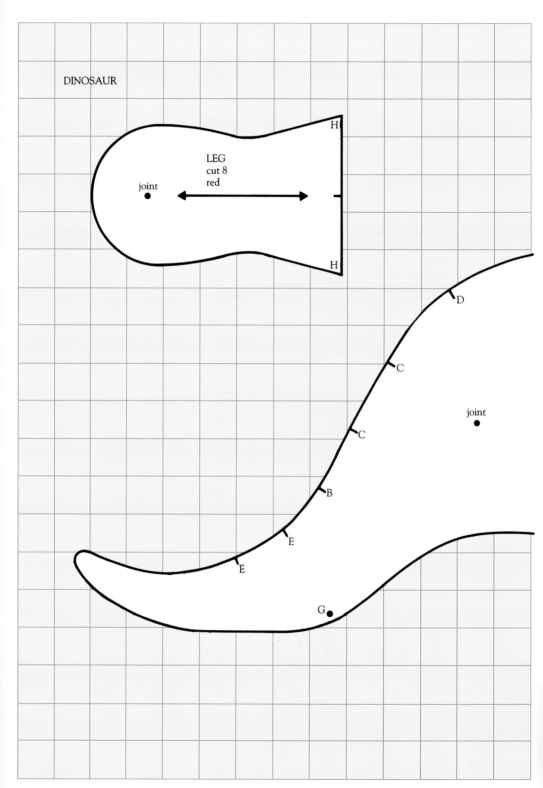

DINOSAUR

LEG
cut 8
red

joint

H

H

joint

D

C

C

B

E

E

G

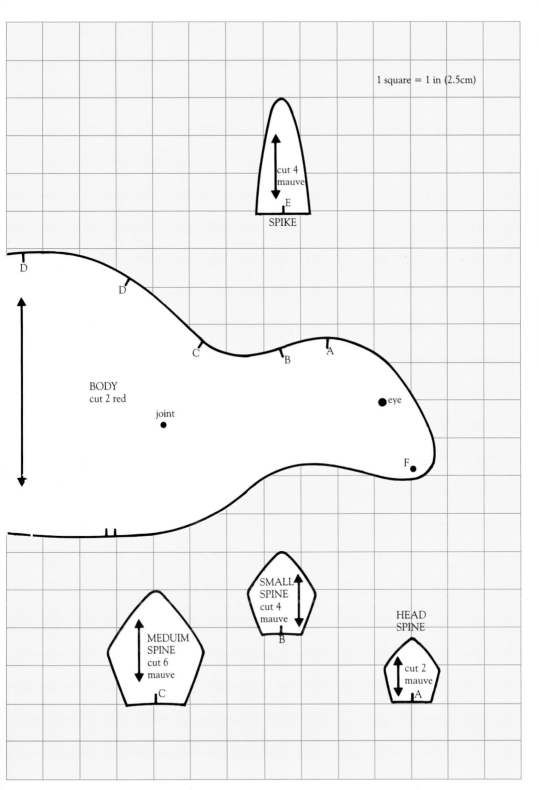

1 square = 1 in (2.5cm)

cut 4
mauve
E
SPIKE

D

D

C

B

A

BODY
cut 2 red

joint

● eye

F ●

SMALL
SPINE
cut 4
mauve
B

MEDUIM
SPINE
cut 6
mauve
C

HEAD
SPINE

cut 2
mauve
A

Making the toy

4 Pin and stitch the spines and spikes together in pairs leaving the ends open.

5 Turn right side out and stuff lightly. Baste across the ends of the spines and spikes then baste to one body shape matching A, B, C, D and E.

6 Pierce tiny holes at the eye and joint positions of the body and 4 of the legs. Pin and stitch the bodies together F–G, passing through A, B, C, D and E.

7 Pin and stitch the gusset to the body F–G–F, leaving an opening to turn. Turn right side out and attach the eyes.

8 Stitch each 'joint' leg to a plain one H–H along the un-notched edges, leaving an opening to turn. Baste and stitch the pads to the legs H–H. Turn right side out. From the inside, insert the stalk of a joint through the hole. Stuff the legs firmly and slipstitch the opening closed. Fix the leg joints through the holes on the body. Stuff the body, taking care to push the filling into the tip of the tail then slipstitch the opening closed.

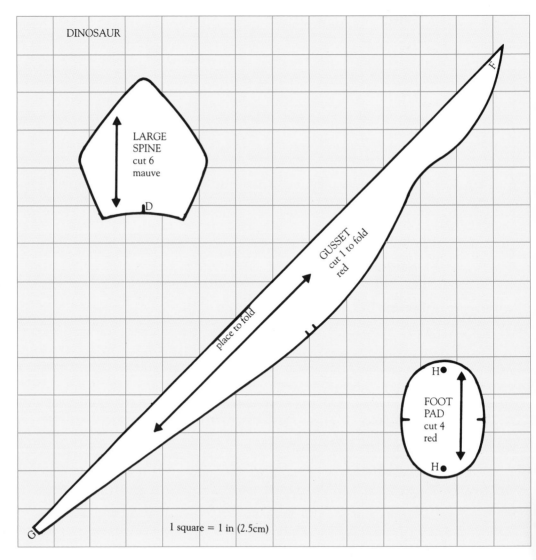

DINOSAUR

LARGE SPINE
cut 6
mauve

D

GUSSET
cut 1 to fold
red

place to fold

F

H●

FOOT PAD
cut 4
red

H●

G

1 square = 1 in (2.5cm)

Edward the elephant

*This smart, striped pachyderm is an ideal size for a toy
and, made from a washable fabric and stuffed with polyester filling, he
will launder easily.*

Materials

20in (50cm) of 36in (90cm)-wide striped
  cotton
4in (10cm) square of white cotton
Two ⅜in (9mm)-diameter buttons
White stranded embroidery thread
Washable polyester toy filling
Large-eyed embroidery needle

Preparation

1 Draw a pattern from the graph pattern on
page 63 and put in the marks, words and
numerals. Cut out the pattern pieces.

2 From striped cotton, cut out 2 bodies, 2
undersides, 1 head gusset, 4 ears and 4
hooves. From white cotton, cut 4 tusks.

Making the toy

3 Stitch the bodies together A–F and B–G.
Stitch the undersides together A–B, leaving
a 3¼in (8cm) gap in the middle. Stitch the
darts on the undersides.

4 Stitch the head gusset between the bodies
G–F–G and the undersides to the bodies
A–C, D–D and C–B. Sew the hooves to the
elephant by hand matching C and D. Turn
the elephant right side out.

5 Thread three 4½in (12cm) lengths of
embroidery thread on to a needle, knot the
ends together and from the inside thread
through to the outside at point A for the
tail. Remove the needle, and plait the
threads. Knot the ends together and fray the
threads below the knot.

6 Stuff the elephant and slipstitch the
opening closed. Stitch the ears together in
pairs, leaving an opening to turn. Turn right
side out and slipstitch the openings closed.
Hand sew a ⅜in (1cm) deep tuck on the
front edges.

7 Stitch the tusks together in pairs leaving
the straight ends open. Turn right side out
and turn in the opening edges for ¼in
(6mm). Stuff firmly, then slipstitch the
opening edges together. Pin the ears, tusks
and button eyes to the face. Hand sew in
position.

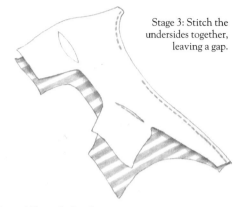

Stage 3: Stitch the
undersides together,
leaving a gap.

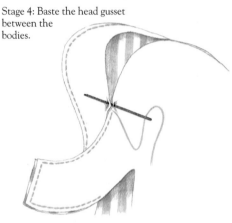

Stage 4: Baste the head gusset
between the
bodies.

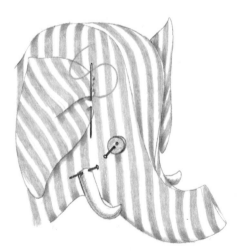

Stage 7: Hand sew the ears to
the face.

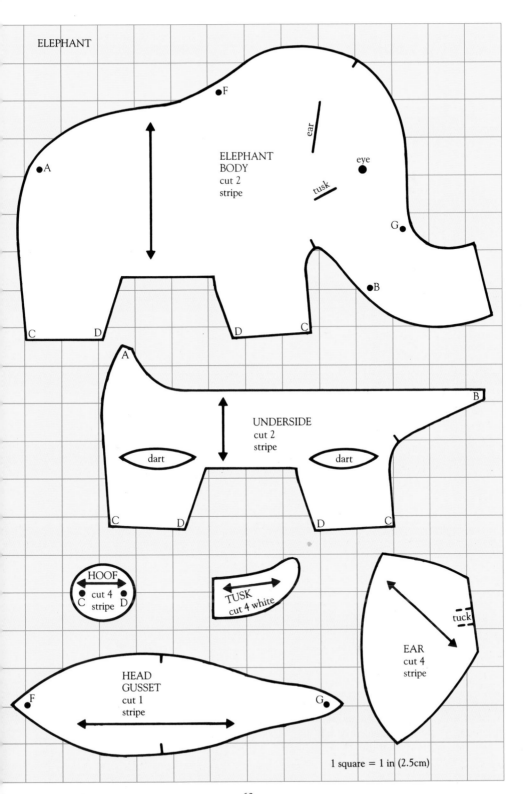

ELEPHANT

ELEPHANT
BODY
cut 2
stripe

ear

eye

tusk

A

F

G

B

C   D   D   C

UNDERSIDE
cut 2
stripe

A

B

dart   dart

C   D   D   C

HOOF
cut 4
stripe
C   D

TUSK
cut 4 white

EAR
cut 4
stripe

tuck

HEAD
GUSSET
cut 1
stripe

F

G

1 square = 1 in (2.5cm)

FOUR

Playmates

Grab toys

These little animal shapes are for young babies and, if you make them of colour-fast, washable fabrics and fill them with a good-quality washable filling, they will be completely safe. Make sure that all seams are properly stitched and thread ends fastened off. Always sew ribbons and ties on very securely.

Materials (for each toy)
8in (20cm) of 36in (90cm)-wide printed
    fabric
8in (20cm) of 36in (90cm)-wide plain fabric
8in (20cm) of ⅝in (15mm)-wide satin
    ribbon (optional)
Scrap of black fabric
Washable polyester toy filling
Bodkin

Preparation
1 Trace the pattern on page 68 and put in all marks, words and numerals. Cut out the pattern.

2 From the plain fabric, cut out 4 ears. From printed fabric, cut 2 bodies on the fold. For the rabbit's bobtail, cut a 2½in (6cm)-diameter circle of plain fabric. For the cat's and mouse's tails, cut a bias strip of plain fabric 4¼in × 1½in (11 × 3.5cm).

Making the toys
3 Stitch the ears together in pairs around the notched edges. Turn right side out and stuff lightly. Baste the raw edges together.

4 Pin and baste the rabbit's ears ⅝in (15mm) apart to the top of one head. Pin and baste the teddy's, cat's and mouse's ears 1¼in (3.5cm) apart to the top of one head.

5 Stitch the bodies together leaving an opening to turn. Turn right side out and stuff lightly. Slipstitch the opening closed. From black fabric, cut two ⅜in (9mm)-diameter circles. Gather edges, turn under, press and then sew to the face.

Stage 4: Baste the toy's ears to the top of the head on one body piece.

Stage 8: Gather the fabric edges, stuff the bobtail and sew to the rabbit.

Use the pattern to make a pram toy. Cut the shapes from stiff Vilene, bond to wrong side of fabric. Make up toy then cut the same shape from fabric. Zigzag shapes together on edges, wrong sides facing. Embroider the features, sew ribbon loop to head.

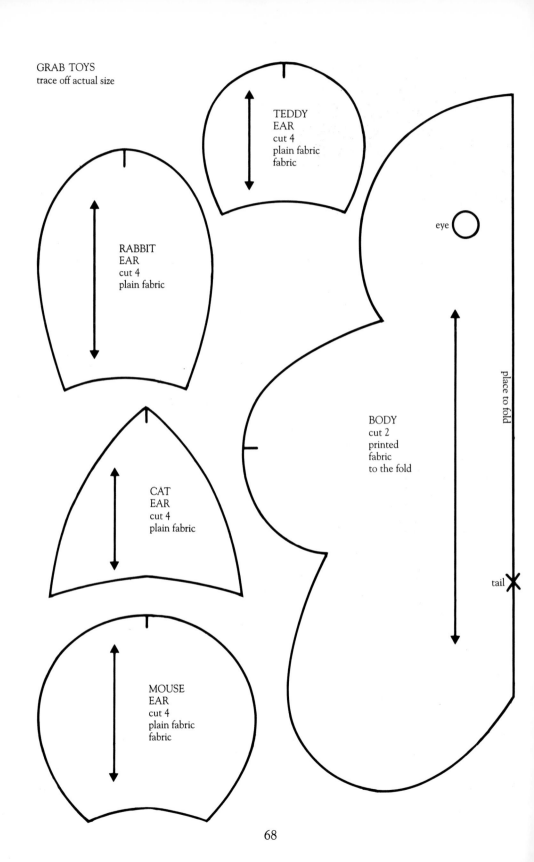

GRAB TOYS
trace off actual size

TEDDY
EAR
cut 4
plain fabric
fabric

RABBIT
EAR
cut 4
plain fabric

eye

place to fold

BODY
cut 2
printed
fabric
to the fold

CAT
EAR
cut 4
plain fabric

tail ✗

MOUSE
EAR
cut 4
plain fabric
fabric

6 Tie the ribbon in a bow and sew securely to the toy. Cut the ends in a fishtail.

7 To make the rabbit's bobtail, turn under ¼in (6mm) on the edges and gather.

8 Pull up the gathers making a shallow bowl shape and stuff. Pull up the gathers tightly enclosing the toy filling. Sew securely to the toy at the place marked with a cross on the pattern.

9 For the cat's and mouse's tails, fold the tails lengthwise in half and stitch along the long edge. Turn right side out using a bodkin. Turn in ¼in (6mm) at the ends.

10 Sew one end of the tail to the toy at the marked cross. Gather the turned-in end tightly and fasten securely.

Mouse house

The two mice who live in this toadstool house are very comfortable but there wouldn't be enough room for even one more mouse!

Materials

Thick card
Thin card
20in (50cm) of 60in (150cm)-wide red felt
8in (20cm) of 60in (150cm)-wide fawn felt
12in (30cm) of 60in (150cm)-wide white felt
8in (20cm) of 60in (150cm)-wide green felt
Scraps of brightly coloured felt for the flowers
Polyester toy filling, Masking tape, Household glue, Fabric glue

Preparation

1 For the top cut out a 10¼in (26cm) diameter circle of thick card. Cut out a 3½in (9cm) diameter circle in the centre. From the red felt, cut out a 17¼in (44cm) diameter circle.

Making the toadstool

2 Sew a gathering stitch around the circumference of the felt circle and pull up the gathers making a shallow bag. Stuff with toy filling, then place the card circle so that the circumference of the felt extends over the card circle for about ¾in (2cm). Fasten the gathers securely.

3 Continue stuffing the toadstool firmly through the hole in the card. Glue the gathers to the card. From the fawn felt, cut a 10in (25cm) diameter circle and glue to the underside.

4 To make a pattern for the stalk, cut a rectangle of paper 15 × 6¼in (38 × 16cm). In the centre, cut an archway 5½in (13.5cm) high and 3½in (9cm) wide. Cut out the stalk in thin card. Pull the card between thumb and finger to curve it, then overlap the ends by 1in (2.5cm) and stick in place with a small strip of masking tape.

5 From the fawn felt, cut out a rectangle 15 × 7½in (38 × 19cm). Wrap it around the stalk with ⅝in (1.5cm) extending at the top and bottom. Overlap and glue the ends at the back with fabric glue.

6 Trim away the felt around the arch leaving a ⅝in (1.5cm) allowance. Snip to the curve and glue the edges to the inside.

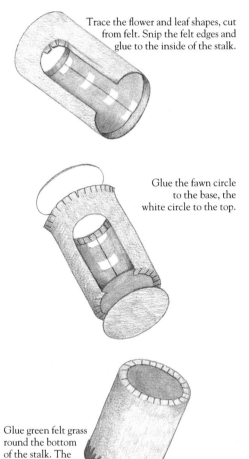

Trace the flower and leaf shapes, cut from felt. Snip the felt edges and glue to the inside of the stalk.

Glue the fawn circle to the base, the white circle to the top.

Glue green felt grass round the bottom of the stalk. The trace-off patterns for the flowers are on page 74.

70

7 To line the stalk, cut out a rectangle of white felt 15 × 6¼in (38 × 16cm). Use the stalk pattern to cut out the archway 2in (5cm) from one end. Starting at one side of the archway, use fabric glue to stick the lining inside the stalk, overlapping the ends.

8 Cut out two 4⅜in (11.2cm) diameter circles in thin card, two from white felt and one from fawn felt. Glue each white felt circle to a card circle.

9 Snip the felt at the top and bottom of the stalk then glue to the card side of the circles. Glue the fawn felt circle under the base. Use the household glue to stick the top of the toadstool centrally on top of the stalk.

10 From the white felt, cut out five 3¼in (8cm) diameter circles and glue to the top of the toadstool. Cut out a strip of green felt 10¾ × 1in (27.5 × 2.5cm) for the grass. Cut out points along one long edge and glue around the base of the stalk.

11 Cut 2 narrow strips of green felt for stems and glue each side of the archway. Cut 4 leaves in green felt (see page 74 for trace-off patterns) and glue to the stems. Cut out 14 hollyhocks in shades of pink felt. Overlap the end petals and glue together. Glue the hollyhocks to the stems. Cut out flowers from brightly coloured felt and glue to the grass. Cut out tiny circles of yellow and green felt and glue to the centre of each flower.

Mr and Mrs Mouse

Here are the owners of the toadstool house on page 70. They are very easy to make and a child who is interested in sewing might enjoy helping to make his own mouse family.

Materials

8in (20cm) square of fawn velvet
8in (20cm) of 36in (90cm)-wide fawn felt
Small amounts of printed fabric and wine
    and blue felt for clothes
Short length of edging lace
Flesh-pink stranded embroidery thread
Thin card
4 small black beads
2 white pearl beads
Black toy whiskers
Polyester toy filling
16in (40cm) of ⅛in (3mm)-wide ribbon
Small artificial flowers
Household glue

Preparation

1 Trace the pattern on pages 74–75. Put in all marks, words and numerals. Cut out the pattern pieces.

2 For each mouse, cut out 2 heads in velvet fabric.

3 From fawn felt, cut out 2 bodies to the fold and 1 base for Mrs Mouse. Cut out 2 shirts from printed fabric, 2 trousers to the fold and 1 base from blue felt.

Making the mouse

4 Stitch heads together leaving the straight edge open. Turn right side out and stuff. Gather the lower, straight edge. Pull up the gathers tightly. Fasten off.

5 Stitch each shirt to a trouser piece. Press under ¼in (6mm) on the upper edges. Stitch the curved edges of the bodies together. Stitch the bases to the bodies, matching fold lines.

6 Cut an 8in (20cm) length of embroidery thread for each mouse, knot one end and thread on a needle through the base seam at the back from the inside. Cut out two bases from card and place inside each mouse.

7 Stuff the bodies firmly and gather the upper pressed edge, place the gathered end of the head inside the body with the head facing forward, pull up the gathers tightly and sew to the head gathers.

8 From printed fabric, cut out 2 dresses to the fold and 2 sleeves for Mrs Mouse. Stitch the dresses together at the side seams and stitch a ⅜in (1cm) hem on the lower edge. Stitch edging lace to the dress with the edge of the lace level with the hemmed edge. Stitch ribbon to the top edge of the lace.

9 Sew edging lace to the upper raw edges, overlapping the ends of the lace at the back. Press under ¼in (6mm) on the upper edges then slip the dress over the body matching side seams. Gather the upper pressed edges to fit the neck and fasten the gathers securely.

10 To make the jacket for Mr Mouse, cut out 2 front jackets, 1 back jacket to the fold and 2 sleeves from wine felt. Stitch the fronts to the back along the notched side seams and press the revers open along the crease lines. Wrap the jacket around the body overlapping the front edges. Sew in place with 2 pearl bead buttons.

11 Press under ¼in (6mm) on the upper and lower edges of the sleeves. Sew edging lace to the printed sleeves edges. Fold the sleeves and stitch together along the raw edges. Turn right side out.

12 Cut out 2 hands for each mouse from fawn felt. Inset the straight end of each hand into the lower edge of each sleeve. Gather the sleeve ends to fit around the hands and sew securely to the hands.

13 Loosely stuff the sleeves with toy filling. Gather the upper edges of the sleeves slightly. Pin the sleeves to the sides of the mice and hand sew to the bodies along the upper gathering.

14 Sew a black bead each side of the head at the eye positions. Pull the thread between the eyes to pinch in the face. Attach 3 whiskers to the face, trim the ends.

15 From fawn felt, cut out 4 ears and 4 feet. Hand sew a pair of ears to the top of the heads and glue the feet under the bases, facing forward.

16 Glue a tiny spray of artificial flowers in Mrs Mouse's hand and a single flower in front of one ear.

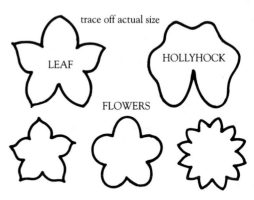

Trace these shapes and cut from felt to decorate the mouse house on page 70.

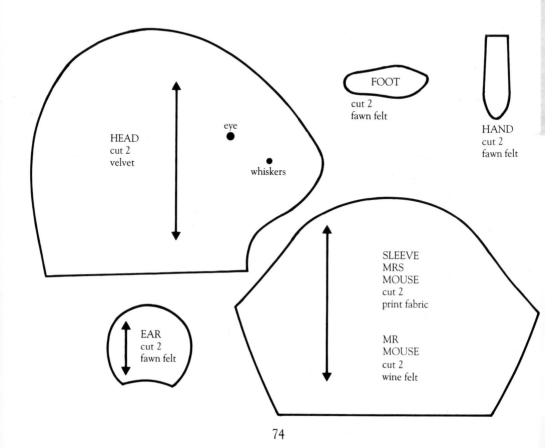

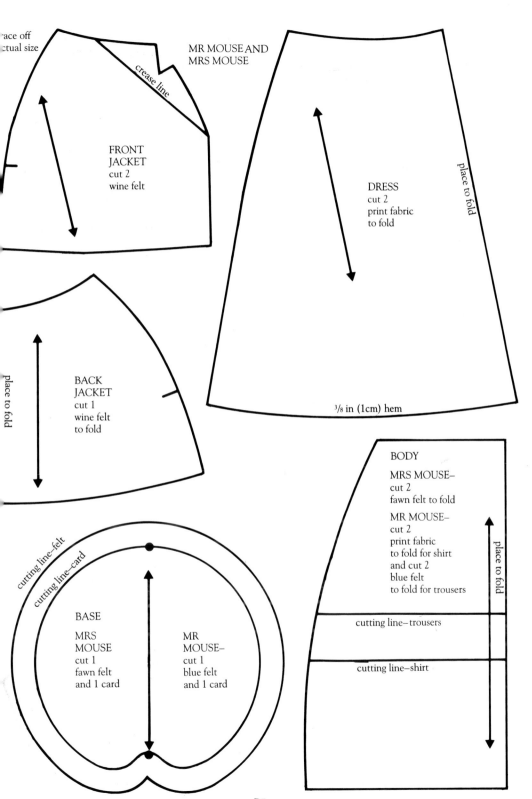

race off
ctual size

crease line

MR MOUSE AND
MRS MOUSE

FRONT
JACKET
cut 2
wine felt

DRESS
cut 2
print fabric
to fold

place to fold

BACK
JACKET
cut 1
wine felt
to fold

place to fold

³/₈ in (1cm) hem

BODY

MRS MOUSE–
cut 2
fawn felt to fold

MR MOUSE–
cut 2
print fabric
to fold for shirt
and cut 2
blue felt
to fold for trousers

place to fold

cutting line–felt

cutting line–card

BASE

MRS
MOUSE
cut 1
fawn felt
and 1 card

MR
MOUSE–
cut 1
blue felt
and 1 card

cutting line–trousers

cutting line–shirt

Easter Bunny

All dressed up in her spring dress and apron, with a flower-trimmed straw hat, Easter bunny is ready for anything, including the Easter Parade. The pattern on pages 78–79 also makes the sleepy mouse.

Materials
12in (30cm) of 60in (150cm)-wide white
    polished fur fabric
9in (23cm) square of apricot felt
Scrap of fawn felt
Thin card
Two ⅜in (9mm) brown toy eyes
Apricot yarn
Toy whiskers
Washable polyester toy filling

Preparation
1 Draw a pattern from the graph patterns on
pages 78–79 on squared paper. Put in all
marks, words and numerals. Cut out the
pattern pieces.

2 From the fur, cut out 2 heads, 1 gusset, 2
body fronts, 2 arms and 2 body backs. Cut
two 4⅝in (12cm) diameter circles for the
bunny's base and tail.

3 Cut 2 outer ears from the fur and 2 inner
ears from apricot felt.

Making the toy
4 Cut 2 irises from fawn felt. Make
holes on the heads at the eye positions then
stitch the heads together A–B. Stitch the
gusset between the heads C–A–C. Turn
right side out.

5 Pierce a hole through the centres of the
irises. Insert the stalk of the eyes through the
iris holes then fix to the heads.

6 Stitch body fronts together B–D and the
arms to the body fronts E–F. Stitch body
backs together G–H, leaving a 4¾in (12cm)
opening to turn. Stitch the side and arm
seams I–F–J. Stitch the head to the body
matching points B and G.

7 Stitch the base to the lower edge of the
bunny. Turn right side out and cut out a
4⅛in (10.5cm) diameter circle of card. Place
inside the bunny on the base. Now stuff the
bunny and slipstitch the back opening
closed.

8 Press under ¼in (6mm) on the lower
edges of the fur and felt ears. Stitch the outer
ears to the inner ears leaving the lower edges
open. Turn right side out and slipstitch the
lower edges together. Fold the ears
lengthways in half with the fur outside. Sew
to the top of the head with the inner ears
facing forward.

9 Gather the circumference of the tail. Pull
up the gathers and place toy filling inside.
Oversew the raw edges securely together
making a round ball. Sew to the back seam
2in (5cm) above the base.

10 Make a large fly stitch at point A with
the yarn. Attach whiskers to each side of the
face and trim to 2in (5cm) long.

Stage 4: Stitch the gusset between the
head pieces, C-A-C.

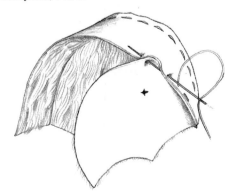

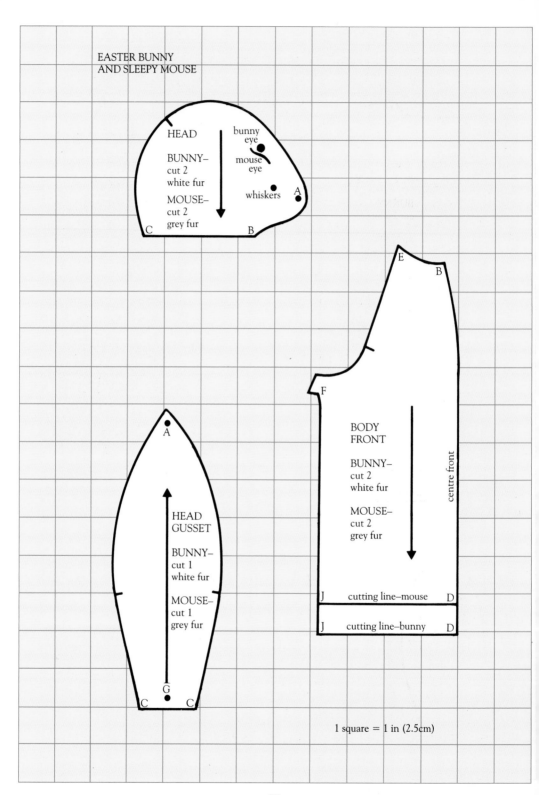

EASTER BUNNY
AND SLEEPY MOUSE

HEAD

BUNNY–
cut 2
white fur

MOUSE–
cut 2
grey fur

bunny
eye

mouse
eye

whiskers

A

C

B

E

B

F

BODY
FRONT

BUNNY–
cut 2
white fur

MOUSE–
cut 2
grey fur

centre front

A

HEAD
GUSSET

BUNNY–
cut 1
white fur

MOUSE–
cut 1
grey fur

G

C   C

J   cutting line–mouse   D

J   cutting line–bunny   D

1 square = 1 in (2.5cm)

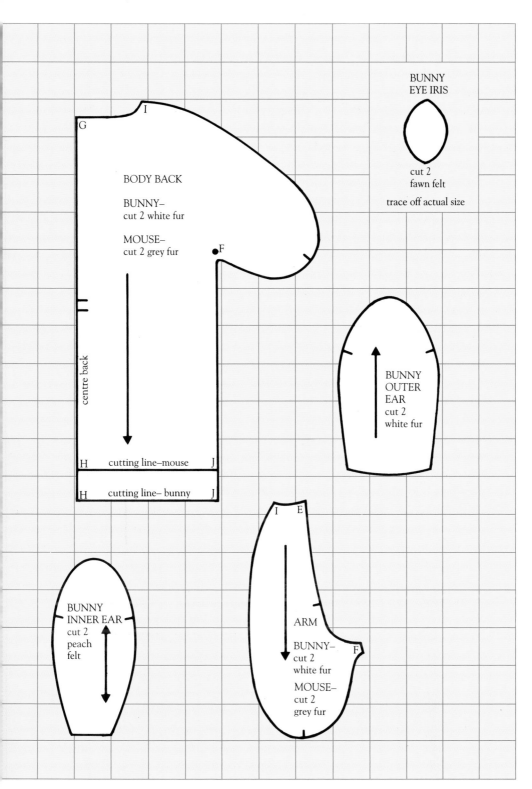

BUNNY
EYE IRIS

cut 2
fawn felt

trace off actual size

BODY BACK

BUNNY–
cut 2 white fur

MOUSE–
cut 2 grey fur

•F

centre back

H   cutting line–mouse   J

H   cutting line– bunny   J

G

I

BUNNY
OUTER
EAR
cut 2
white fur

BUNNY
INNER EAR
cut 2
peach
felt

ARM

BUNNY–
cut 2
white fur

MOUSE–
cut 2
grey fur

I   E

F

79

BUNNY'S CLOTHES

Materials
12in (30cm) floral fabric
12in (30cm) white cotton fabric
1½yd (1.5m) scalloped edging lace
28in (70cm) narrow edging lace
1⅛yd (1m) of 1in (2.5cm)-wide edging lace
1⅛yd (1m) of ⅛in (3mm)-wide ribbon
2 press fasteners
Apricot raffia, small silk flowers

Preparation
1 Draw a pattern from the graph pattern on pages 82–83, on squared paper. Put in all marks, words and numerals. Cut out the pattern pieces.

2 From the floral fabric cut out 1 front to the fold, 2 backs, 2 sleeves and a strip for the skirt 21½ × 5in (55 × 12.5cm). Stitch the front to the backs at the shoulder seams. Stitch the narrow edging lace to the neck edge. Turn under ⅜in (9mm) on the back edges and stitch in place. Overlap the backs by ⅜in (9mm) and tack across the lower edges. Stitch the side seams.

3 Stitch a ⅜in (9mm) hem on the sleeves, stitch the narrow lace to the lower edge with the ribbon ¼in (6mm) above. Stitch the underarm seams. Gather sleeves between the dots and stitch to the bodice, matching side and underarm seams and dots to the shoulder seams.

4 Baste the scalloped edging lace to one long edge of the skirt on the right side, keeping the lower edges level. Stitch along the inner edge of the scallops. Trim away the fabric under the scallops. Stitch a row of ribbon ⅜in (9mm) above the scallops. Gather the wide edging lace and stitch to the lower edge of the scallops, overlapping the ends at the back.

5 Stitch the skirt ends together leaving a 3in (7.5cm) opening for the tail ⅝in (15mm) above the lower edge. Gather upper edge of the skirt and stitch to the lower edge of the front and back with the seam at centre back. Sew back opening on the press fasteners.

Apron
6 From the white fabric, cut out 1 upper apron, 2 straps to the fold, 1 lower apron 4⅝in × 4in (12 × 10cm), 2 ties 16 × 2in (40 × 5cm) and 1 band 3½ × 2in (9 × 5.5cm). Apply the scalloped edging to both of the short and 1 long edge of the lower apron. Gather the upper edge and stitch to one long edge of the band, ¼in (6mm) in from the ends. Press under ¼in (6mm) on the opposite long edge.

7 Cut one end of the ties diagonally. Narrowly hem the long and diagonal edges. Gather the straight ends to ¾in (2cm) and baste to the ends of the band. Fold the band lengthways in half with right sides facing and stitch across the ends. Turn the band to the right side and slipstitch the long edges together, enclosing the apron seam.

8 Apply the scalloped edging to the longest edge of the upper apron. Fold the straps in half along the fold line with wrong sides facing and baste on top of the upper apron matching the strap fold lines to the broken lines. Apply the scalloped edging to the long raw edges of the straps.

9 Hand sew the lower edge of the upper apron and straps behind the band. Sew the ends of the straps to the ties 4¾in (12cm) from the gathers.

10 To make the bonnet, cut six 90in (230cm) lengths of raffia. Knot together at one end and divide into 3 sets of 2 strands and plait. Knot together at the ends. Starting at one end, coil the plait in a circle, slip-stitching the edges together as you go. Continue until it is the same size as the inner circle on the bonnet template pattern (see pages 82–83).

11 Now follow the shape of the template, leaving a gap for the ears each side of the inner circle. When complete, cut off the plait end and oversew to the underside. Sew silk flowers to the front.

Sleepy mouse

This dozy toy would make anyone want to go to bed and it may be just the thing for a child who likes to stay up far too late. The mouse is made from the same pattern as the Easter bunny, with adaptations.

Materials

12in (30cm) of 60in (150cm)-wide grey
    polished fur fabric
7in (18cm) square of pink fabric
Thin card
Pink and black stranded cotton embroidery
    thread
Black toy whiskers
16in (40cm) pink cord
Toy filling
Clear nail varnish

Preparation

1 Cut paper pattern following the
instructions for the Easter bunny on pages
78–79, adapting the pattern for the mouse as
instructed.

2 From the fur fabric, cut out 2 heads, 1
gusset, 2 body fronts, 2 arms and 2 body
backs.

3 Cut out 2 ears from the fur and 2 from the
pink fabric.

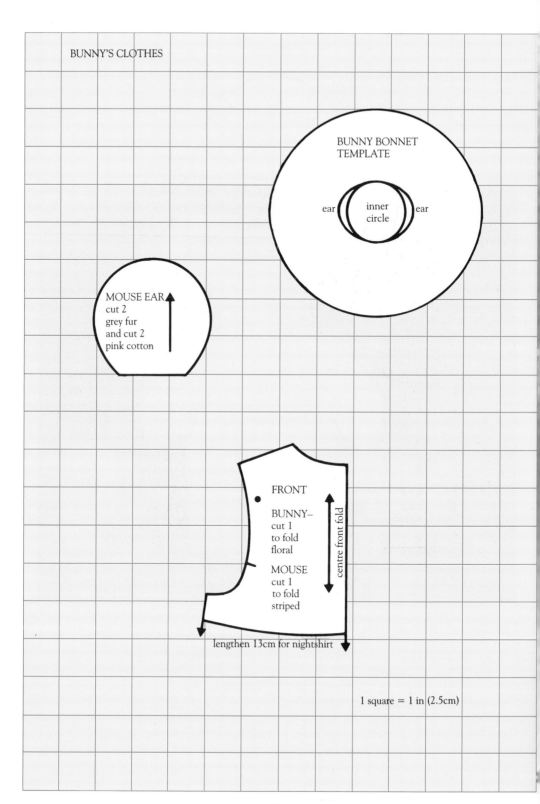

BUNNY'S CLOTHES

BUNNY BONNET
TEMPLATE

ear inner
circle ear

MOUSE EAR
cut 2
grey fur
and cut 2
pink cotton

FRONT

BUNNY–
cut 1
to fold
floral

MOUSE
cut 1
to fold
striped

centre front fold

lengthen 13cm for nightshirt

1 square = 1 in (2.5cm)

82

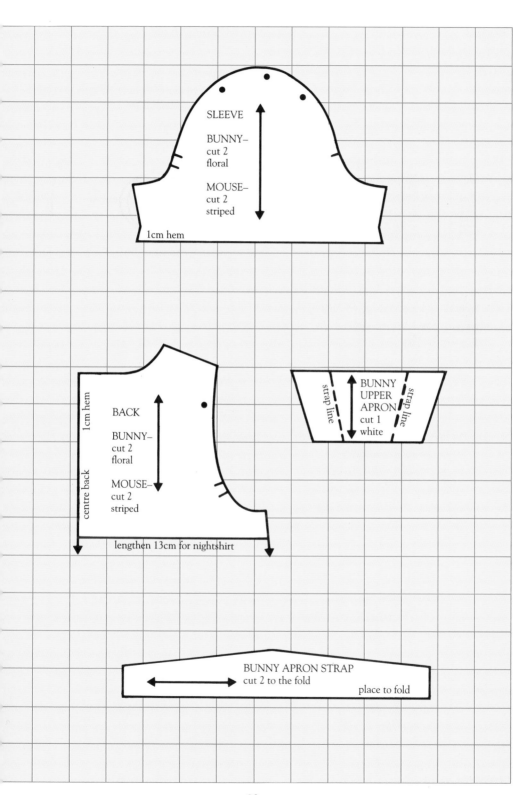

SLEEVE

BUNNY–
cut 2
floral

MOUSE–
cut 2
striped

1cm hem

BACK

BUNNY–
cut 2
floral

MOUSE–
cut 2
striped

1cm hem

centre back

lengthen 13cm for nightshirt

BUNNY
UPPER
APRON
cut 1
white

strap line

strap line

BUNNY APRON STRAP
cut 2 to the fold

place to fold

Making the toy

4 Stitch the heads together A–B. Stitch the gusset between the heads C–A–C. Turn right side out.

5 Follow the instructions for the Easter bunny, stage 6, then baste the end of the cord to the back seam for a tail and follow Easter bunny's stage 7.

6 On the ears, press under ¼in (6mm) on the lower edges and stitch together in pairs. Turn right side out and slipstitch the pressed edges together. Sew ears to the top of the head. Work a large fly stitch at point A (see pattern) with pink embroidery thread.

7 Embroider the closed eyes with black embroidery thread in stem stitch. Dab nail polish on the end of the tail. When it has dried, cut diagonally across the varnished area, this will stop the end fraying.

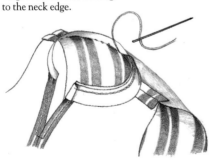

Stage 3: Stitch bias binding to the neck edge.

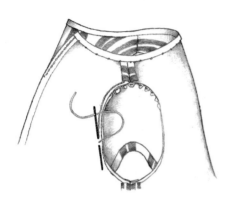

Stage 4: Stitch the gathered sleeves to the nightshirt.

MOUSE'S CLOTHES

Materials

(40cm) of 36in (90cm)-wide striped cotton
12in (30cm) white bias binding
3 small white buttons
1 press fastener
White stranded embroidery thread

Preparation

1 Draw patterns from the graph patterns on pages 82–83, on squared paper. Put in all marks, words and numerals. Cut out the pattern pieces.

2 Cut out 1 front to the fold, 2 backs and 2 sleeves. To make a pattern for the nightcap, draw a triangle on paper 7in (18cm) long and 7in (18cm) high. Cut out and use as a pattern to cut 2 nightcaps.

Making the clothes

3 Stitch the front and backs together at the shoulder seams. Stitch the back seam starting 4in (10cm) below the neck edge and taking ⅜in (1cm) seam allowance. Press under ⅜in (1cm) on the back opening edges and stitch in place. Stitch bias binding to the neck edge. Turn to the inside and stitch in place.

4 Stitch the side seams. Stitch the underarm seams of the sleeves and stitch a ⅜in (9mm) hem on the lower edges. Gather the sleeves between the dots and stitch to the nightshirt matching the side to the underarm seams and dots to the shoulder seams.

5 Make a ⅜in (9mm) hem on the nightshirt and fasten the neck with a press fastener.

The best teddy

A true, traditional teddy bear that everyone will love – and he has a growler inside – so beware!

Materials

20in (50cm) of 54in (137cm)-wide sand-
coloured Super Lush beaver fur fabric
8in (20cm) square of sand-coloured velvet
8in (20cm) of 44in (114cm)-wide printed
fabric
Two ⅝in (15mm) black toy eyes
¾in (18mm) black cat nose
Washable polyester toy filling
Toy growler

Preparation

1 Draw a pattern from the graph pattern on
pages 90–91, on squared paper. Put in all
marks, word and numerals. Cut out the
pattern pieces.

2 From the fur fabric, cut out 2 heads, 1
gusset on the fold, 2 fronts, 2 backs, 2 arms
and 2 legs.

3 Cut 2 ears from the fur fabric and 2 from
the velvet. Cut out 2 soles from velvet.

4 From the printed fabric, cut a strip
40 × 4¾in (105 × 12cm).

Making the toy

5 Stitch the heads together A–B then baste
the gusset between the heads D–C–A–C–D.
Snip to the dots at C and stitch as basted.

6 Make a tiny hole at the eye and nose
positions and attach the eye and nose.

7 Stitch the fronts together B–E. Stitch the
backs together F–E, leaving an opening to
turn to the right side. Stitch the front and
back together along the shoulder seams
G–H.

8 Stitch the head to the body B–G–B.
Stitch the arms to the body J–H–J. Then
stitch the crotch seam M–E–M and the
underarm seam L–J to the dot on the arms.

9 Fold the legs in half and stitch N–O.
Stitch the soles to the legs matching O and

P. Hand sew the legs to the body L–M–N–L.

10 Turn the teddy right side out and stuff
the head, arms and legs. Start to stuff the
body, laying the filling against the front and
back. Place the growler inside then continue
stuffing the body. Slipstitch the opening
closed.

11 Stitch each fur ear to a velvet ear,
leaving the lower edge open. Turn right side
out and turn ¼in (6mm) on the lower edge
to the inside. Oversew the folded edges
together and hand sew to the top of the head
with the velvet side towards the front.

12 Fold the fabric strip lengthways in half
and cut the ends diagonally. Stitch along the
ends and long edge leaving an opening to
turn to the right side. Turn right side out
and press. Tie in a bow around teddy's neck.

Stage 8: Stitch the bear's
head to the body.

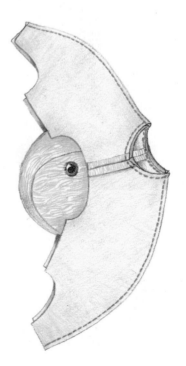

Sailor panda

Pandas are well-known the world over and for many years they have rivalled teddy bears in popularity.

Materials

20in (50cm) of 60in (150cm)-wide white
    polished fur fabric
16in (40cm) of 60in (150cmm)-wide black
    polished fur fabric
Two ⅝in (15mm) amber toy eyes
Scrap of black felt
Black stranded embroidery thread
Washable polyester toy filling

Preparation

1 The pattern is adapted from the teddy
bear pattern on pages 90–91. Follow the
instructions for adapting the pattern. Cut
out the pattern pieces.

2 From the white fur fabric, cut 2 heads, 2
fronts, 2 backs and 1 gusset on the fold. From
the black fur fabric, cut 2 arms, 2 legs, 2 soles
and 4 ears. Cut 2 eye patches. Cut a nose
from black felt.

3 Stitch the heads together A–B then baste
the gusset between the heads D–C–A–C–D.
Snip to the dots at C and stitch as basted.

4 Pierce a tiny hole at the eye positions on
the heads and in the patches. Pin the
patches to the head matching the holes and
fur pile. Attach the eyes and remove the
pins.

5 Make up the panda in the same way as the
teddy.

Stage 4: Stitch the sleeves
to front and back.

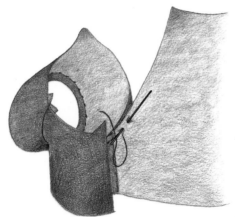

6 Turn the panda right side out and stuff.
Slipstitch the opening closed. Stitch the ears
together in pairs leaving the lower edge
open. Turn right side out and turn ¼in
(6mm) on the lower edge to the inside.
Oversew the folded edges together and hand
sew to the top of the head. Sew the nose and
eye patches to the head. Embroider the
mouth with 3 strands of embroidery thread
using stem stitch.

PANDA'S CLOTHES

Materials

28in (70cm) of 36in (90cm)-wide blue fabric
12in (30cm) of 36in (90cm)-wide white
    fabric
24in (60cm) of ⅝in (15mm)-wide black
    ribbon
1¼yd (1.10m) of ¼in (6mm)-wide white
    braid
20in (50cm) of ¼in (6mm)-wide elastic
White yarn
2 press fasteners
Bodkin

Preparation

1 Draw a pattern from the graph patterns on
pages 92–93 on squared paper. Put in all
marks, words and numerals. Cut out the
pattern pieces.

2 From the blue fabric, cut 2 jacket fronts, 1
jacket back on the fold, 2 sleeves and 2
collars. Cut 2 trousers.

3 From the white fabric, cut 4 shoe uppers
on the fold, 4 tongues and 2 soles.

Making the toy

4 Stitch the jacket fronts and back together
along the side seams. Stitch the underarm
seam of the sleeves and stitch a ⅜in (9mm)
hem on the lower edge. Stitch the sleeves to
the front and back.

5 Stitch the collars together along the outer
edges and turn right side out. Baste the raw
edges together. Hand sew the white braid
¼in (6mm) inside the outer edges of the
collar and ¼in (6mm) above the sleeve
edges.

6 Baste the collar to the neck edge matching the fold lines and dots. Fold the facings to the outside and baste to the neck edge. Cut a bias strip of blue fabric 12 × 1¼in (30.5 × 3cm). Fold and baste lengthways in half with the right side outside and stitch to the neck edge.

7 Turn under the ends of the bias strip, turn the strip and facing to the inside and slipstitch to the jacket.

8 Hand sew a ⅜in (9mm) hem on the lower edge. Tie the ribbon in a bow and hand sew to the front. Cut the ribbon ends in a fishtail. Slip the jacket onto Panda and overlap the front edges. Sew on press fasteners.

Stage 6: Baste and stitch the bias strip to the neck edge.

9 Fold trousers in half and stitch the inner leg seams. Stitch the centre front and back seams matching the inner leg seams. Make ⅜in (9mm) hems on the lower edges.

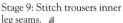

Stage 9: Stitch trousers inner leg seams.

10 Turn ⅜in (9mm) to the inside on the upper edge. Stitch in place, leaving an opening to insert the elastic. Thread the elastic through with the bodkin and adjust to fit. Sew the ends of the elastic together securely.

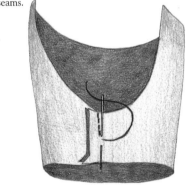

11 Stitch the shoe uppers together in pairs along the notched edges. Pierce small holes at the crosses. Baste the uppers to the soles matching the dots.

12 Stitch the tongues together in pairs along the notched edges. Turn right side out and baste the lower edges together. Baste the tongues to the soles matching the dots at the front. Stitch the sole seams. Turn right sides out.

13 Slip the feet into the shoes and fasten with the white yarn threaded through the holes in the uppers.

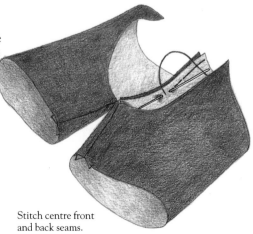

Stitch centre front and back seams.

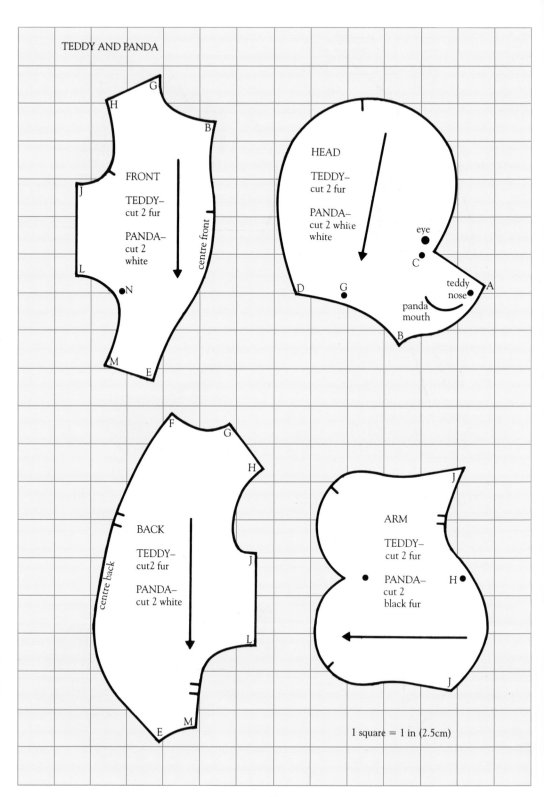

TEDDY AND PANDA

FRONT

TEDDY–
cut 2 fur

PANDA–
cut 2
white

centre front

HEAD

TEDDY–
cut 2 fur

PANDA–
cut 2 white
white

eye

teddy
nose

panda
mouth

BACK

TEDDY–
cut2 fur

PANDA–
cut 2 white

centre back

ARM

TEDDY–
cut 2 fur

PANDA–
cut 2
black fur

1 square = 1 in (2.5cm)

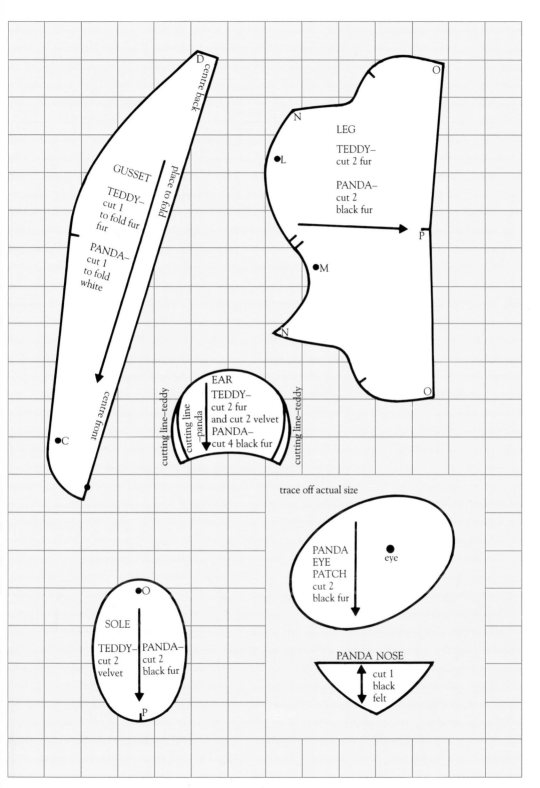

GUSSET

TEDDY–
cut 1
to fold fur
fur

PANDA–
cut 1
to fold
white

D

centre back

place to fold

centre front

●C

LEG

TEDDY–
cut 2 fur

PANDA–
cut 2
black fur

N

O

●L

●M

N

O

P

EAR
TEDDY–
cut 2 fur
and cut 2 velvet
PANDA–
cut 4 black fur

cutting line–teddy

cutting line
–panda

cutting line–teddy

trace off actual size

PANDA
EYE
PATCH
cut 2
black fur

● eye

SOLE

TEDDY–
cut 2
velvet

PANDA–
cut 2
black fur

●O

P

PANDA NOSE

cut 1
black
felt

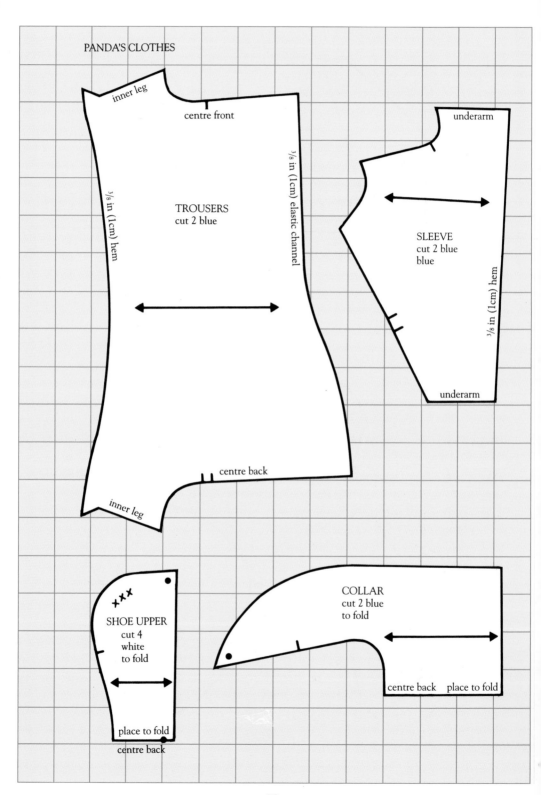

PANDA'S CLOTHES

inner leg

centre front

3/8 in (1cm) elastic channel

TROUSERS
cut 2 blue

3/8 in (1cm) hem

centre back

inner leg

underarm

SLEEVE
cut 2 blue
blue

3/8 in (1cm) hem

underarm

SHOE UPPER
cut 4
white
to fold

place to fold

centre back

COLLAR
cut 2 blue
to fold

centre back   place to fold

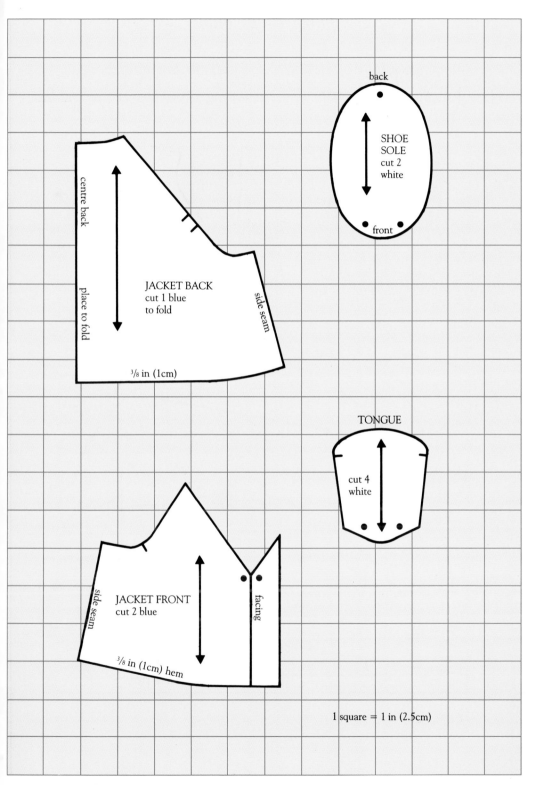

back

SHOE
SOLE
cut 2
white

front

centre back

place to fold

JACKET BACK
cut 1 blue
to fold

side seam

³/₈ in (1cm)

TONGUE

cut 4
white

side seam

JACKET FRONT
cut 2 blue

facing

³/₈ in (1cm) hem

1 square = 1 in (2.5cm)

Flippy the dolphin

Another much-loved creature, and sadly in danger in the seas.
However, this toy looks happy and will bring lots of pleasure to children
of every age.

Materials
16in (40cm) of 36in (90cm)-wide pale blue
  fabric
16in (40cm) of 36in (90cm)-wide cream
  fabric
12in (30cm) square of dark-blue fabric
Two ⁵⁄₁₆in (7mm) black toy eyes
Black stranded embroidery thread
Washable polyester toy filling

Preparation
1 Trace the pattern and put in all marks,
words and numerals. Cut out the pattern.

2 From the dark-blue fabric, cut out 6 fins
and 2 tails. From the pale blue fabric, cut 2
bodies. From the cream fabric, cut 1 under
body on the fold.

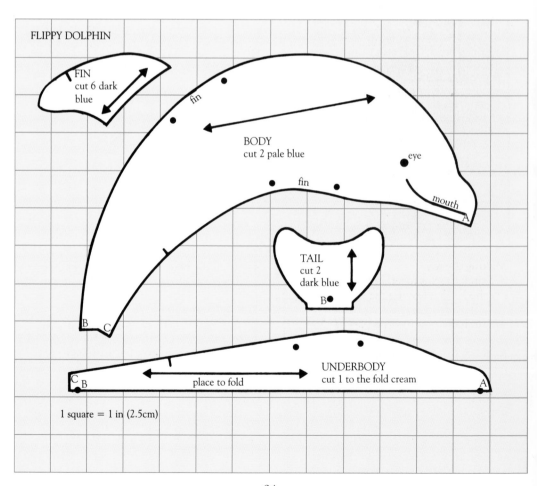

FLIPPY DOLPHIN

FIN
cut 6 dark
blue

fin

BODY
cut 2 pale blue

eye

fin

fin

mouth

A

TAIL
cut 2
dark blue

B

B   C

C   B

UNDERBODY
cut 1 to the fold cream

A

place to fold

1 square = 1 in (2.5cm)

Making the toy

3 Stitch the fins together in pairs along the notched edges, leaving the lower edges open.

4 Stitch the tails together, leaving the straight edges open. Turn the fins and tail right side out and stuff lightly. Baste the raw edges together.

5 Make tiny holes at the eye positions. Tack 2 fins to the lower edge of the bodies between the dots, with the points facing away from the head. Baste the remaining fin to the top of one body between the dots, with the point facing away from the head.

6 Stitch the bodies together A–B. Fix the eyes in position.

7 Stitch the under body to the bodies C–A–C leaving an opening to turn. Insert the tail into the end of the dolphin matching points B. Stitch across the end then turn the dolphin right side out.

8 Stuff the dolphin and slipstitch the opening closed. Embroider the mouth along the broken lines with 3 strands of embroidery thread, using stem stitch.

95

Useful addresses

For fur fabrics, felt and toy-making
components:

Beckford Mill
Prince Street
Dudley Hill
Bradford BD4 6HQ

Dainty Toys
Unit 35
Phoenix Road
Crowther Industrial Estate
District 3
Washington
Tyne and Wear NE38 0AB

For toy-making accessories and felt:

The Handicraft Shop
Northgate
Canterbury
Kent CT1 1BE

The author and publishers would like to
thank The Handicraft Shop, Northgate,
Canterbury, Kent for their help in compiling
this book.